We Don't Make
Widgets

We Don't Make
Widgets

Overcoming the Myths That Keep
Government from Radically
Improving

Ken Miller

GOVERNING MANAGEMENT SERIES
Governing Books, Washington, DC

Published by Governing Books
A Division of Governing Magazine
1100 Connecticut Ave., NW, Suite 1300
Washington, DC 20036

www.governing.com

Cover and interior design: Naylor Design, Washington, DC

∞ The paper used in this publication exceeds the requirements of the American National Standard for Information Sciences—Permanence of Paper for Printed Library Materials, ANSI Z39.48-1992.

Printed and bound in the United States of America

11   10   09   08   07   2   3   4   5

Library of Congress Cataloging-in-Publication Data

Miller, Ken, 1970–
    We don't make widgets: overcoming the myths that keep government from radically improving/Ken Miller.
        p. cm.—(Governing management series)
    Includes index.
    ISBN-13: 978-0-87289-480-8 (alk. paper)
    ISBN-10: 0-87289-480-0
    1. Government productivity—United States. 2. Administrative agencies—United States—Management. 3. Organizational change—United States. I. Title.
    JK468.P75M55 2006
    351.73—dc22
                                                    2006025367

Contents

v

Preface

Discovery consists of seeing what everybody has seen and thinking what nobody has thought.

—*Albert Szent-Györgi von Nagyrapolt*

I have spent my life improving government. Not because I enjoy repeatedly smacking my head against a brick wall but because improving government is—to me—one of the most rewarding fields of endeavor. Shaving a few pennies off a manufacturing process or developing a better widget that can be sold at higher margins just doesn't get me going in the morning. But helping a child abuse hotline protect kids by adopting the rigorous protocols of a 9-1-1 center or giving mental health patients and their families greater control over their care are causes worth fighting for.

I have been a regulator, a planner, a deputy director of a large state agency, the leader of a statewide transformation effort, and a government consultant. I have worked alongside the best and the brightest from every type of agency at every level of government. I've worked in the welfare office and the governor's office. I have experienced the joy of watching two thousand staff members make radical improvements for their customers and being recognized nationwide for their efforts. I've experienced the pain of watching a new administration telling these same staff members to get back in their cages. This is my life's work and—for better or worse—I love it.

I have also spent time out of government working with corporations and manufacturers, large and small. They've taught me amazing things that I can't wait to share with you. The impact their ideas will have on your agency is unbelievable.

The purpose of this book is to radically improve government by changing the beliefs of the managers who run it. Beliefs are powerful. Beliefs drive our behaviors. Beliefs can change the world. And it is my contention in this book that it is our beliefs that stand in the way of the progress we all want to make.

What we believe about government—that we don't make widgets, that we don't have customers, and that we're not here to make a profit—all feed the bigger myth: that we're different. That somehow the improvements everybody else is making can't possibly work here. That what we do is unique. And that the modern industrial movement of the past quarter century has no relevance to our day-to-day operations.

This is not a patronizing run-government-like-a-business book. In many cases I believe businesses should be run more like governments. (Can you imagine if corporations were as frugal with their investors' money as we are with the taxpayers' dollars?) Rather, consider this book a Rosetta stone—a way to finally crack the code to the world of performance improvement that so often gets lost in translation.

 BOX P.1 Who Is a Manager?

In this book I'll lump executives, directors, deputy directors, bureau chiefs, assistant bureau chiefs, assistants to the assistant bureau chief, managers, and supervisors into one category—managers.

Government will radically improve when we see the world in a different way—free of the myths. We will improve government when we

- recognize we do make widgets and that what we do can easily be measured, managed, and improved

- see our work as the factories that make these widgets and we discover how to use the same tools that industry uses to make our factories run 80 percent faster and at lower cost

- discover that we have real customers, with all the rights and privileges that the word "customer" bestows, and that our customers are not who we think they are and that their satisfaction is absolutely essential to our success

- learn that we are here to deliver a return to our investors and are responsible for figuring out innovative ways of achieving better results with fewer resources.

Then perhaps we can dispel the greatest myth of all—that government managers are somehow inferior to their private-sector counterparts. From what I've seen, the only thing inferior is the paycheck.

Acknowledgments

I have had the pleasure of working for and with a lot of great people in my life. One of the greatest honors has been my longtime friendship and association with Robin Lawton. His concepts, introduced in his groundbreaking 1993 book *Creating a Customer-Centered Culture: Leadership in Quality, Innovation and Speed,* shaped my worldview and have proved to be the most effective way to create lasting, radical improvement. Robin's book, videos, and workshops all drive home the critical components necessary to create a customer-centered culture. (Please see the Appendix for a list of these components.) These concepts are at the heart of customer-centered culture change and are the foundation of my philosophy and hence this book. I encourage you to visit www.imtC3.com to learn more about the concepts, strategies, and tools of Robin Lawton's *Creating a Customer-Centered Culture.*

Special Thanks

I would like to thank all the people who have made this book possible.

To my wife, Jennifer: Thank you for your unconditional love. Thank you for keeping our lives together when I am away. Thank you for waiting for me. I am, and will forever be, *here*.

To my best friends and collaborators, Blake Shaw and Bill Bott: Blake, you give me the confidence to take on the world. Your belief and tireless effort have made everything possible. Bill, thanks for the ideas and edits that kept this book alive. Your humor and insight were invaluable. I am blessed to have both of you and your families in my life.

To my father, whose lifelong passion to improve government rubbed off on me despite my best efforts to avoid it.

To American Airlines, for all the air-sickness bags they lent me (on which to capture my ideas).

To the Case family, for letting me use their beautiful lake home while I wrote this book.

To the good people at *Governing*, who have believed in me from the beginning—especially Roger Wilson and Elder Witt. I am humbled by your support.

And, most important, to the change agents who have been fighting the battles every day, who begged me for a book they could give to other people so that they would "get it." This book is for you. Pass it on.

We Don't Make
Widgets

Chapter

The Three Myths

If there was a big gardening convention, and you got up and gave a
speech in favor of fast-motion gardening, I bet you would get booed
right off the stage. They're just not ready.

—*Jack Handey*
Deep Thoughts

I live in a capital city and have spent my career improving government either inside the walls as an employee or outside the walls as
a consultant. As I watch yet another set of elected officials take
office with what they think is the completely novel idea of improving government by eliminating waste, fraud, and abuse, I am
reminded of that quotation often attributed to Albert Einstein:
"Insanity is doing the same thing over and over again and expecting
different results." Of course the newcomers think their initiatives
will be different—different blue-ribbon commissioners, different
consultants, and new and innovative forms to be filled out—but the

result will be the same. "Another tune on the triangle," as Peter Scholtes says.[1] No doubt the pressure to improve government is at an all-time high. (This timeless sentence will be true whenever you read this book.) This pressure is especially intense given the radical improvements made at lighting speed by the world's top companies.

There is pressure on us to cut costs ...

A desktop computer now costs less than $400. A DVD player or a microwave oven can be purchased for the price of a large pizza with the works. Yet the cost of government always seems to be going up. It's not that we aren't trying, but how do we cut costs when most costs are out of our control? How do we save money when we don't even know what things cost? How do we cut costs when all our costs are salaries?

There is pressure on us to improve customer satisfaction ...

I stayed at a Westin hotel in Canada once and was able to get them to make a 5 a.m. wake-up call. Big deal? The call wasn't for me. They called my wife, two time zones away, to make sure she was up for an important meeting. Yet we can't get anyone in government to even answer the phone.

It's not that we aren't trying, but how can we improve customer satisfaction if we don't admit we have customers? How do we improve customer satisfaction when we have multiple customers with competing interests? How can we possibly give customers what they want when we can barely afford to give them what they need?

There is pressure on us to be less bureaucratic and work faster ...

It used to take weeks to get approved for a mortgage; now it takes seconds. Purchasing music used to mean waiting for the album to

---

[1] Peter R. Scholtes, *The Leader's Handbook: Making Things Happen, Getting Things Done* (New York: McGraw-Hill, 1998).

arrive in the store and driving there to pick it up; now we can have it the minute the song is finished.

In government offices, customers wait in line for hours to apply for food stamps and for weeks to get them. Businesses wait months or years to get crucial building permits, and tax refunds arrive just in time to pay taxes again.

It's not that we aren't trying, but how can we go faster when we don't have the resources to keep up now? How can we go faster if we don't know how long things currently take? How can we go faster when we don't have control over the laws and regulations?

There is pressure on us to prove results ...

Corporate America is not only responsible for delivering ever-increasing value to shareholders. Companies are also accountable for the accuracy of their forecasts and the reliability of their data.

In government we are able to show how much we spend and what we spend it on, but we struggle to show the results. It's not that we aren't trying, but how do you prove a result that may not happen for another ten years? How do you take sole credit for a result when you might be just one of twenty variables? How do you measure the results of prevention—like crimes that didn't happen and buildings that didn't fall down?

Are we defective?

How is it that the private sector does so well at these things and government struggles so mightily? Are we defective? Are we missing a chromosome? Have all the slow, inefficient, customer-hating people in the world found a home in government?

I have conducted workshops with government managers at every level—federal, state, county, city, and even foreign governments. I start each workshop the same way—with a challenge: As a team they have been assigned responsibility for a manufactured product (sometimes a Ford Mustang, sometimes a cell phone, sometimes a wristwatch). The company that makes it is in trouble, and the team has to turn it around. They have fifteen minutes to figure out what they would want to know in order to plan the turnaround. Before you look on the next pages, try it yourself. What would you want to know about a Ford Mustang plant you just inherited?

In fifteen minutes or less, every group comes up with at least the following:

- the number of orders for the cars
- the number of cars produced (and whether the plant kept up with orders)
- the time required to produce a car
- the cost to produce a car
- staff turnover on the line
- the percentage of cars that roll off the line with defects
- customer satisfaction with the car
- repeat customers
- market share
- profit

With another five minutes, they are able to put a number or a percentage in front of their responses. What do they have? A robust set of performance measures—a balanced scorecard for a place they've never seen. They can manage. In fact, what they come up with is exactly what you would find on the shop floor if you visited those plants.

System-of-Work Measures

These government managers are amazing. In fifteen minutes they develop measures to help them decide their financial health—today and in the future. They find a way to measure costs and to pinpoint what might be driving those costs. They understand their customers and begin to think about how to segment their market with unique offerings. They understand supply and demand and what constrains their capacity. Simply, they have the information to radically improve that plant.

At the end of this exercise, I ask the basic question: "How is it possible to create a balanced scorecard in ten minutes for a place where you've never worked, yet many of you have worked in your jobs for ten years and don't measure and manage any of the things on the list?" The excuses come flying:

- We don't make widgets.

- We're not here to make a profit.

- We don't have customers.

- Our survival doesn't depend on customer satisfaction.

- We get penalized for being efficient.

- It's easy when you have a factory; we're in the service business.

- People don't want what we produce; we make them have it.

- The people who pay for our services are not those who use it.

- But we have elected officials. ...

- There is no incentive for us to improve.

- Government was created to be inefficient—a swift government is a totalitarian government. (This one is always my favorite.)

(Feel free to add your own excuses to the list.)
These excuses fall into three general categories:

1. **We don't make widgets.** What we do is hard to describe, squishy, intangible service stuff. Therefore we can't really measure it, manage it, or improve it.

2. We don't have customers. We have hostages—they didn't choose us, they don't want to come back, and it doesn't really matter if they are happy or not. Also, we have multiple customers with competing interests who can never agree on what they want versus what they need.

3. We're not here to make a profit. There is no incentive to improve, and any improvements we do make just get taken away from us anyway.

These are the three myths that keep government from radically improving.

Myths are mental constructs that are not true. These mental constructs obscure reality, and they lead to unfortunate consequences. If you still believe in Santa Claus (I hope I didn't just ruin that for you), you will misplace your gratitude. If you believe in the myth that everyone on public assistance is out to cheat the system, you will devise cumbersome controls on 100 percent of the customers to guard against the 4 percent of bad actors. If you believe in the myth that employees are naturally lazy and only want to get by doing the minimum, you will waste enormous energy on performance management schemes like pay for performance, performance appraisals, and incentive systems.

The three myths—we don't make widgets, we don't have customers, and we're not here to make a profit—prevent us from seeing the reality of our organizations. Simply put: organizations, both public and private, are collections of systems. Systems are processes (including the inputs, suppliers, and employees who work in the processes) that produce widgets for customers in order to achieve some desired result or outcome. The way we improve an organization is to improve its systems. Let's explore this a little further.

System of Work

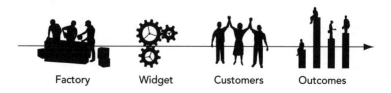

| Factory | Widget | Customers | Outcomes |

BOX 1.1   System of Work and Purpose

W. Edwards Deming introduced the concept of work as a system; he called it his SIPOC model: suppliers, inputs, process, outputs, customers. Many have rightly pointed out that this model was missing a key element—purpose. A system exists to accomplish two sets of purposes (or outcomes), those the organization desires and those the customer desires. Robin Lawton's customer-centered culture model (in *Creating a Customer-Centered Culture: Leadership in Quality, Innovation, and Speed*, published in 1993) includes both the organization outcome and the customer outcome, and it also brings some rigor to the language of outputs and customers. It is from these two masters, and others, that the system-of-work model used in this book is derived.

No matter which industry you are in, you use the same model—the system of work—to get things done. The system to produce a widget—in this case, a Ford Mustang—makes intuitive sense to anyone. Ford obtains from its suppliers numerous inputs such as steel, tires, and glass. Employees working in the factory convert these inputs into the widget—the Mustang. The Mustang is in turn sold to

System of Work for a Ford Mustang

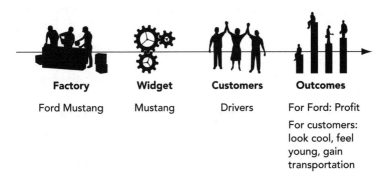

Factory	Widget	Customers	Outcomes
Ford Mustang	Mustang	Drivers	For Ford: Profit
			For customers: look cool, feel young, gain transportation

a customer. All of this occurs for two reasons: The first is the outcome Ford wants from all of this—profit. The second is the outcome the customer wants from the Mustang—to go fast, to look cool, to recover lost youth, and, incidentally, to get from point A to point B.

Ford has developed sophisticated initiatives to measure, manage, and improve every interaction in the system. Ford works aggressively with suppliers to ensure that high-quality inputs arrive just in time. Ford reengineers the factory to make it work as fast as possible, all the while minimizing waste and defects. Ford works with customers to find out exactly what they want (lots of cup holders) and then builds that into the widget. Ford tracks profitability and continually looks for new widgets to create what will make even more money.

Again, no matter the industry, it uses the same model—the system of work—to get things done. The system for an industry that doesn't appear to make widgets, doesn't appear have customers, and doesn't exist to make a profit—a church, in this example—also makes sense. It turns out that churches and ministers actually do make widgets (they are called sermons, wedding ceremonies, and funeral services), they do have customers, and they are here to make a profit—it's just not measured in dollars (depending on your denomination).

System of Work for a Religious Sermon

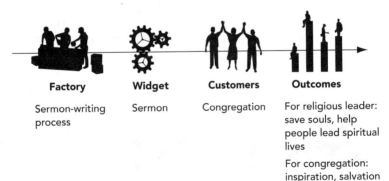

Factory	Widget	Customers	Outcomes
Sermon-writing process	Sermon	Congregation	For religious leader: save souls, help people lead spiritual lives
			For congregation: inspiration, salvation

Do you suppose the church is using the same sophisticated initiatives that Ford uses to measure, manage, and improve every interaction in the system? Yes, supplier relations are a little difficult in this scenario, but when was the last time your place of worship conducted a focus group to determine the drivers of your satisfaction for sermons?

These same concepts apply to government—for example, in the system for protecting kids by means of child abuse investigations.

System of Work for a Child Abuse Investigation Report

Factory	Widget	Customers	Outcomes
Investigation of child abuse	Child abuse investigation report	Prosecutors	For human services agency: safe kids, strong families For prosecutors: safe kids, successful prosecution

Do you suppose human services agencies work with prosecutors to uncover the lawyers' expectations for the report? (More on this in chapter 4.) Do you suppose the human services agencies have reengineered the process to increase capacity and minimize variance and errors? Do you think they measure how many investigation reports are correct the first time? Usually not.

Why not? The three myths. They don't see the systems. Instead they see piles of rules, regulations, and policies. They see staffing issues, resource constraints, and living conditions we can't imagine. What they don't see is the way out, which is the focus of this book.

Organizations are collections of systems. Literally hundreds of systems—systems big and small, systems that feed other systems—are producing hundreds of widgets inside the walls of your organization's building.

Systems to Protect Children from Abuse

Laws	Hotline protocols	Hotline call	Investigation report	Prosecution case

Pop the top off your government building and you will see an amazing thing—hundreds of factories churning out widgets for customers in an effort to achieve results. How do we improve an organization? Improve those systems. (But not all at once. See chapter 6.) Unfortunately, we in government just don't see the systems because we are blinded by the myths. And these three myths drive the biggest myth of all for government: that we're different

- because we don't make widgets, and what has been done to improve productivity in factories doesn't apply in government;

- because we don't have customers in the traditional sense, and what has been done to develop innovative new products that delight customers isn't relevant to us;

- because we're not here to make a profit, and we don't have to worry about coming up with the next innovation first.

 BOX 1.2 **Government Systems**

Government systems include the following:

arrests	gallons of water
audit reports	GED programs
bridge repairs	job-training programs
budgets	laws
building permits	parks
child abuse investigations	probation visits
code inspections	purchase orders
collections	regulations
company relocation	restaurant inspections
proposals	tax refunds
computer repairs	treatment plans
driver's licenses	unemployment checks
educational standards	vaccinations
environmental permits	zoning ordinances
filled potholes	

We cordon ourselves off from the vast store of knowledge about how to improve. Instead, we continually turn to ourselves and to those like us for new ideas. Agency after agency continues to attend conference after conference with each other, and we keep reinventing the same playbook.

Another saying attributed to Einstein—"The significant problems we face cannot be solved at the same level of thinking we were at when we created them"—reminds us we have to look further. Because we believe we are different and because we don't see the systems, we've come up with some amazingly ineffective (all right, I'll say it—crazy) ways to create change. The next chapter will show you how to avoid the big mistakes.

 MPA ↟ MBA?

How pervasive is this thinking that we are different? So much so that we have our own advanced degree—a master's in public administration (MPA). Apparently what they teach in master's of business administration (MBA) programs won't work in government. Also, apparently, an MPA won't get you a job as a plant manager. I hope this book will solve both of those problems.

Chapter 2

The Amazingly Ineffective (Crazy, Actually) Ways Government Tries to Improve

In a comedy routine, Jerry Seinfeld asks, "Why is it that when men see a pretty woman in traffic they honk their horn? Do they really think the woman is going to stop what she is doing and get in? At no time in the history of man has this ever worked, yet men keep honking. Why? It's the best idea they've come up with."

The same is true with our government reform initiatives. They never actually work, yet we keep on honking. Here are some of my favorites:

The Blue-Ribbon Commission

Imagine that you are the shareholder of a large company and a new chief executive officer (CEO) has been hired. When the CEO was asked how she was going to make the company great, she responded "I'm going to form a blue-ribbon commission comprising retired government executives and professors as well as consultants who have never worked in our sector. We are going to have this esteemed panel fly over our factories at about 30,000 feet and then, using their expertise, they will tell us how we can be more efficient and effective." Heck, for the fun of it, let's throw some investors onto that commission as well. What would you do? I'd sell my shares as fast as possible.

Yet this is how most government reform efforts begin—with a blue-ribbon panel of people who don't understand how government works and also, amazingly, forget that the purpose of an organization is to achieve a higher return for its investors by building better widgets for customers in more efficient factories.

Here is a real-life example of the brilliance that comes out of these commissions. This comes from a real questionnaire sent by a real blue-ribbon commission to agency executives. Ask yourself how you would answer these four questions:

1. Are there functions your division/agency performs that may be considered by some to provide little value for the time and costs incurred?

2. What functions in your division/agency could be more effectively and efficiently performed? What can be done to improve their effectiveness and efficiency?

3. What functions in your division/agency could be more effectively and efficiently performed by another department?

4. What functions in your department are duplicative either within your department or across other agencies?

What do we get from these commissions? A thick report that basically tells people to stop using cell phones and cars, to automate everything that isn't automated, and to centralize everything that is decentralized (until the next commission, which will advocate decentralizing everything this commission centralized).

You can't improve government by looking at it from 30,000 feet. The problems with government aren't visible at that level. It's only when you open up the roof and see the factories inside that you can find the opportunities. Improving government is a battle that is won on the ground, not through the air.

The Politburo

What some people call the "politburo" are the central planners who lurk in the hallways of budget and planning divisions across the land. Their dream is a simple one:

> If only we could link every dollar, every move, every bathroom break, and every copy machine to the objectives of the unit, which are perfectly in sync with the goals of the division, which are tightly aligned with the ...
>
> (Wait a minute! we've already used goals and objectives. What term can we use now? How about *outcome*? No, wait! We need to save that for later. Perhaps we could say *intermediate outcome*, which could feed multiple outcomes that culminate in the end outcomes. Brilliant!)

Of course, their dream is that elected officials will look at the tightly woven logic of the budgets and plans and be able to instantly see how each of their decisions will affect the citizens who elected them. The elected officials will then put aside partisan politics, preconceived biases, and constituent horror stories and make their budget decisions based solely on the facts. Their dreams do come true—in fantasyland.

I once started a project to see whether the cost of creating a budget this way actually outstripped the size of the discretionary dollars that were being allocated. The politburo sent the project to Siberia.

The politburo, like the performance management KGB, are government re-formers. That is, they believe that there is no problem in government that we can't fix with a better form. If we can redo the form, we can change government. The politburo tries to re-form managers. The performance management KGB tries to re-form employees.

I am a reformed member of the politburo. I was the principal architect of Missouri's "Show Me Results" system. This elaborate system linking agency performance to statewide indicators was one of the first in the nation, and it helped the state of Missouri receive one of only two grades of A awarded by *Governing* magazine in the managing-for-results category. On paper, the system was beautiful, the envy of every Myers-Briggs INTJ in the land. However, when push came to shove and budgets had to be cut, how were decisions made? Politics.

One side forced cuts in education spending to make the other side look like the devil. Funding was cut to the environmental agency because of delays in certain construction permits. You know how this works. Were there positives to come out of the initiative? Sure. Departments worked together on common goals, the aims of government were a little more visible, budget people excelled at creative writing. But I'm not convinced these things wouldn't have happened anyway, or that they justified the burden the planning produced.

"Show Me Results" failed at its two primary purposes: to help elected officials make more informed choices about where to invest taxpayers' money, and to help agencies improve. I'm convinced that nothing will help the former. And, as far as the latter, my belief is simple—you can't plan your way to change. Planning is nothing more than intent, or wishing. Václav Havel, the great reformer of communism in the Czech Republic, is said to have stated: "Vision is not enough, it must be combined with venture. It is not enough to stare up the steps, we must step up the stairs." Communism fell because there was no way the central planners could ever outperform freedom.

Reorganization

For whatever reason, reorganizations are usually the first play out of the playbook. They are the inevitable recommendation of every blue-ribbon commission. Reorganizations happen at every level of every organization. New management; new organization chart. My brother worked for a large computer maker that isn't Dell and went through five reorganizations in four years. New management, new structure. As I'm writing this, one state in our great nation is going through a major reorganization (headed by a blue-ribbon commission, of course) for the bold, strategic reason that ... there hasn't been a reorganization in the past 30 years.

Why do we do this? I have a theory that I developed while playing LEGOs with my daughter. Organizational charts are a lot like LEGOs. They are made up of lots of little boxes that you can stack together, break apart, and combine with new ones. You feel like you are building something. You are creating. The almighty power of the creator is in your hands (OK, I'm getting carried away). But the point is, reorganizations are like executive LEGOs. They allow us to

BOX 2.1 Not Enough Chiefs

A state transportation department got itself in an awful bind. A gasoline tax was approved by citizens to fund a 15-year wish list of projects. Unfortunately, halfway into the plan the agency ran out of money. After a great hue and cry, the elected officials decided that there was an "accountability problem" with the department and something had to be done. They astutely diagnosed that the agency was run by a chief engineer—someone who had spent more than thirty years designing and building roads. Surely the problem was that this man knew too much about roads and not enough about money.

So they reorganized the department, creating a chief financial officer to run the department together with the chief engineer. After three years, no new roads had built themselves and no new money had magically appeared, so the elected officials embarked on their second plan—another reorganization. You see, the problem with the agency was that it was being run by two people, which simply couldn't work. So a chief executive officer was brought in to lead the chief financial officer and the chief engineer. At last the roads would be smooth and a four-lane highway would reach every corner of the state. After three years, no

feel as if we've made an improvement when in fact all we've made is a change. (Never confuse the two.)

Will this ever stop? The following quote should cheer you up. Read the date twice.

> We trained hard ... but it seemed that every time we were beginning to form up into teams, we would be reorganized. I was to learn later in life that we tend to meet any new situation by reorganizing; and a wonderful method it can be for creating the illusion of progress

new roads had built themselves and no new money had magically appeared, so the elected officials embarked on their third plan—another reorganization. You see, the problem with the agency was that it reported to an appointed commission. The CEO really needed to report directly to the governor so there would be some real accountability. This led to the creation of a blue-ribbon panel to study the issue further. The panel's recommendation? To reorganize—only this time the members of the commission didn't say how, just that it needed to happen.

So, how do roads build themselves and how does new money magically appear? By improving the systems of the organization, by improving the way roads are scoped, designed, bid, contracted for, maintained, and supervised.

One fine manager from this same organization launched an aggressive initiative to take another look at the scope and design of all the roads cited in the state's transportation plan. With the goal of practical engineering, the organization set out to remove all extraneous elements from road designs (for example, the group replaced an elaborate retaining wall with natural land gradation) and found innovative ways around costly impediments. The result? Savings that equaled a gas tax of 3¢ per gallon for five years. Now, if only they had made that guy the chief.

while producing confusion, inefficiency, and demoralization of our subordinates.

Petronious Arbiter
Grecian Navy
210 B.C.

I hope you won't question my patriotism, but isn't this exactly how we responded to the tragedies of September 11, 2001? We reorganized, created a Department of Homeland Security, and now we're all safer.

The problem with reorganizing is that it doesn't improve the systems of the agency. It just changes where those potentially dysfunctional systems reside.

Focus on Individuals   *individual vs system*

Finally, when all the other ways to improve government have failed, we place the blame squarely where it should be: on the people. We just haven't found the right way to "hold 'em accountable." We're all familiar with this type of change strategy: It's the "we're okay, you're not" philosophy. That is, "the organization would be doing great if you all could just get your act together and do a little more a lot better."

Underlying initiatives like performance appraisals, performance management, training, personal development plans, and suggestion systems (and on and on) is the assumption that improved individual performance will lead to better organizational results. There are some cases where this is so (sales organizations, for example), but in most cases it reveals a fundamental ignorance of how work is done. Individuals work in systems. Poor performance can usually be traced to the system first. W. Edwards Deming's famous estimate was that 96 percent of problems can be attributed to the system and 4 percent to the people. Let's fix the system first.

Perhaps an example will help illustrate this point. The following diagram shows five sequential steps in a process as well as how much each step can produce a day. Because of the complexities of the jobs, each step may differ in length. At the end of the day, how many units can the organization produce? Seventy-five.

Performance Management

Number of widgets produced per day

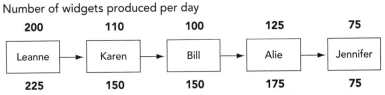

Number of widgets produced per day after performance management changes

Now, let's implement a popular individual-level change initiative—performance management. We sit down and meet with each person individually to develop goals and performance plans for the year. The far right of the figure on the previous page shows the new goals. Now, how many units can the organization produce? Seventy-five.

 Taming the Beast

I once worked on a project in an office that employees called "The Beast." This office had chewed up and spit out some of the best managers I have ever met. Employee dissatisfaction was high, and turnover was out of control. Management and employees had reached an informal stalemate: neither talked to the other. It was no surprise to discover that this office was also the highest source of customer dissatisfaction, rework, cost overruns, and complaint calls from customers.

So, where might a manager start? Boost the employees' pay? Hold a management-employee powwow to create a shared vision? No. None of these would have changed the system of work that was causing all these ill effects. The process would still have ten handoffs. The work would still be simplified to the point where it had no meaning. Customer expectations would still be unclear and unmet. Experience has shown that improving the system and, therefore, improving customer satisfaction and organizational outcomes ends up improving employee satisfaction.

In The Beast, all ten handoffs were eliminated; the ten functions were consolidated into one that required more judgment and increased skills. The result was a process that was 80 percent faster, with a 50 percent drop in errors; employees were more satisfied because their jobs involved human functions like decision making, collaboration, and research; and—lo and behold!—they received higher pay because their work showed increased complexity.

What happened to all the increased productivity? It's sitting in a pile in front of Jennifer. So what do we do next? Well, of course we create a performance goal for Jennifer to reduce the size of the backlog. This ridiculous cycle continues in perpetuity. Rather than the focus being on the individual performers in the process, the focus should have been on how to fix the system: eliminate the process bottleneck, reduce process time, and so on. Then the focus can shift to the skills and productivity of individuals.

Noted sage Peter Scholtes wrote:

> All of the empowered, motivated, teamed-up, self-directed, incentivized, accountable, reengineered, and reinvented people you can muster cannot compensate for a dysfunctional system. When the system is functioning well, these other things are all just foofaraw. When the system is not functioning well, these things are still only empty, meaningless twaddle.[1]

Individual-level change is built on some long-held, faulty assumptions and myths: basically that employees are not giving it their all, and it is management's job to motivate them to do so. Most managers would never admit that this is what they are trying to do, but it is at the heart of every "people program."

This motivation usually comes in two flavors—positive and negative. Most people would say that they abhor negative reinforcement. The era of the boss who yells at people, throws things, and embarrasses people is supposedly over (although I sure do seem to meet a lot of these types anyway). Instead, we've become a kinder and gentler management corps. We use the enlightened techniques of positive reinforcement—employee of the month, a recognition event, gold coins that can be cashed in for prizes, pay for performance, or even a good old-fashioned pat on the back. What we fail to see is that both techniques, positive and negative, are two sides of the same flawed coin.

Anyone who has ever had a new puppy can understand these theories. When you first get a puppy, you have a natural desire for it to fulfill its natural desires outdoors rather than on your carpet.

---

[1] Peter R. Scholtes, *The Leader's Handbook: Making Things Happen, Getting Things Done* (New York: McGraw-Hill, 1998).

Deciding that you will be an enlightened manager of this puppy, you set about using all of your best positive reinforcement techniques. You have special "treats" ready to reward the dog's success, and you use happy, positive language and generally make a great fuss out of anything that looks like progress. Then your patience slowly wanes as you spend yet another half hour on your hands and knees cleaning up another of your puppy's accidents. You then interject some negative reinforcement—a spray bottle of water, a newspaper swat to the behind, a tantrum or two—until you finally reach a shame spiral of disgust. One simple question here: Who is motivated? You or the dog? As Frederick Herzberg would say: You are motivated, the dog is moved.[2]

The same thing happens every day with managers and employees. We continue to search for new techniques to motivate people (quick tip: all those motivational books by successful sports coaches say the same stuff over and over again), whether it's throwing fish, casual Friday, or 360-degree feedback.

The truth is that we can't motivate people. We can definitely move them, but motivation is about energy sources. The most powerful motivation is a limitless energy source—intrinsic motivation—that is inside people. When this engine is firing, we need do nothing but point it in the right direction.

Extrinsic motivation is finite. It comes from outside of us. When we as managers are providing the motivation, we are doing all the work. We are moving all of the pieces. You can choose to work this way but it will wear you out.

Many will argue that pay is a great motivator. It's not. It's a tremendously strong extrinsic mover—once. Then you have to do it again and again and again, at exponentially higher amounts, for it to have any effect. Today's reward is tomorrow's expectation. Think about it for yourself. If I doubled your pay tomorrow would you work harder? Better? Money is not a motivator, but unfair pay can be a lethal demotivator.

For many managers it is a great relief when they realize that it is not their job to motivate Bob. Instead, it is their job to ensure those factors that demotivate Bob (or get in the way of his intrinsic moti-

---

[2] Adapted from the writings of Frederick Herzberg.

vation) are removed and that the system Bob works in has been optimized to ensure excellent performance whether Bob, Ted, or Carol is working in it.

Does this mean we should not recognize employees? Should we not try to inspire them to greatness or help them be all that they can be? Of course not. We just need to understand why we are doing these things. Are we doing them as one friend would to another, or are we doing them as a new owner would to a puppy?

So why do we in government focus so much attention on individuals? Because we can't see the systems! The systems are invisible as long as we are blinded by the myths. After we remove the myths, the systems will appear out of thin air, and we can set about the

---

BOX 2.3 How to Drive Your Staff Crazy— Example 1

A government unit responsible for collecting delinquent payments from customers was having a lot of trouble. The staff had fallen years behind in its work, and employees were buried under a pile of staff grievances. Why? In an effort to increase collections, management had decided that staff needed to be "held accountable." So individual staff members were measured by how much money each brought in the door. Raises, promotions, and dismissals were all based on this metric.

Unfortunately, the staff had absolutely no control over the result. Cases were assigned at random. One employee could be assigned twenty customers ready to pay, with a value of $100,000. Another employee could be assigned twenty customers who had no intention of paying, with a value of $10,000. To make things worse, whether a customer paid or not had nothing to do with the individual behavior of each employee. Employees were trapped in a system they didn't create and couldn't change, and they were being hammered for their unit's poor performance.

---

hard, but rewarding, work of making them the best they can be. It is then quite amazing to see what employees can accomplish in systems that work.

Technology

One of the simplest ways to look like a hero in government is to launch an automation project. These usually have grand names and catchy acronyms and are heralded like a cure for cancer. However they have a dubious side effect: all change in the organization is officially put on hold until the new system is up and running. "Why, it would be silly to make that modification now when the new system will take care of that when it comes online in two years." Of course, ten years later, when the new system is finally ready (and now obsolete), the "hero" has left town and the new management team is left explaining why the project took twice as long and cost three times as much.

 Don't Keep Track—Keep Up!

One of the easiest ways to spot a ripe performance improvement project is to look for anyone installing an automated tracking system. If your process is so messed up that you need a computer system to keep track of how far behind you are, no technology is going to help.
Fix your process!

Am I against technology? Absolutely not, I say (while charging my iPod). I'm just against technology for technology's sake. One time I found myself in an absurd argument with a gentleman; it went something like this:

Me: Why do you want to automate this?
Him: Because it's manual now.
Me: Why is that a problem?
Him: Because it's not automated.

Technology projects in government have such a horrific track record that it's amazing they ever happen. The technology vendors have to be happy that government executives turn over as frequently as they do because a long memory would not serve them well. It's not just their extraordinary cost and their guaranteed tardiness that make them so destructive. It's the impact they have on real improvement. A friend of mine refers to information technology projects as "paving cow paths." That is, instead of boldly clearing new land—creating a new, more efficient process—IT projects tend to pave the old cow paths. The process is just as slow and unresponsive to customers as always, only now it's automated.

Technology can be a great tool to help support initiatives that radically improve the key systems of government. When technology becomes the initiative itself, it inevitably lets everyone down.

Why do we keep doing these things? How do we stop this madness and radically improve government? Achieve more with less? Become customer focused? Run better, faster, cheaper?

We have to bust the myths.

The good news is that to change, all we have to do is change our minds. It doesn't require a $20 million IT solution.

What Works

This book is not a theory book full of musings over the proper role of government. Neither does it espouse a grand new way of budgeting that will instantly turn elected officials into rational decision makers. I will not be extolling the virtues of privatization or introducing any radical policy reforms that will end poverty.

This is a practical book that focuses on improving the performance of government. That is, rather than describing a government that could be or should be, we're going to talk about how to improve the government we already have. Government agencies are collections of systems that have evolved over decades. To improve the agency, to achieve our outcomes, we have to improve these systems—there simply is no other way. Unfortunately, we don't see the systems because we're blinded by the myths.

So, what works?

What works is a group of committed managers who see past the myths and who are working with teams of employees to improve the vital systems for the betterment of the organization, its customers, and employees.

Chapter

We Don't Make Widgets

How would you manage differently if you ran a factory?

L et me illustrate how powerful the "We don't make widgets" myth is. I was involved in some radical reforms at a state agency responsible for collecting taxes and running the Department of Motor Vehicles (DMV). In fewer than three years, working with some amazing people, we

- reduced the time it took to issue tax refunds by 80 percent, and we did it at a lower cost (becoming the fastest in the nation);

- cut wait times in motor vehicle offices by half; in most cases customers were in and out in fewer than fifteen minutes;

- slashed citizens' costs of dealing with bureaucracy.

These reforms were made possible by improving the widget factories inside the organization:

- the tax refund factory

- the driver's license factory

- the car titling factory

- the business audit factory

I was asked by a state governor to share with his state's social services–human services agency how we made these improvements. Two minutes into the presentation, I saw one of the executives giving me the evil eye. It was clear he was not enjoying my presentation in any way. I stopped and asked him, "Sir, am I wasting your time?" To which he responded, "Absolutely. What you've done at a revenue department has no bearing on the type of work we do here. You people are [and this is an exact quote ...] little widget makers. You have little factories that process paper and send out checks. We're here to help families and children."

Being the glutton for punishment that I am, I continued questioning him.

"Explain how you help families?"
"We provide access to health care," he said.
"And how does that work?" I asked.
"Well, we enroll and reimburse doctors for treating low-income patients."
"And how does that work?"
"Doctors submit a form, we process it, and then send them a check."
"I can see how that is nothing like the revenue department," I replied ironically.
"We also protect kids," he hastily replied.
"And how does that work?"
"By supporting foster parents."
"And how do you do that?"
"The foster parents submit a form, we process it, and send them a check."
"Hmm," I said out loud.

At this point, the rest of the room understood. But this gentleman (I actually admire him a great deal) wasn't finished. We went program by program through his department, and what did we find?

Hundreds of factories producing hundreds of widgets (not all of them checks of course). He just couldn't see them. All government agencies do essentially the same stuff; they just do it for different reasons or different outcomes. Yes, the mission of social services is loftier than the mission of the revenue collectors, but once you get inside the factories, they sure look a lot alike. And nobody's been trained to manage them.

The moral of this story is that because he (and most of his agency) couldn't see the widgets and couldn't see the factories, they also weren't improving them.

- Wouldn't kids be better off if we improved the selection of foster parents?

- Wouldn't kids be better off if foster parents could get paid on time, accurately, and with less hassle?

- Wouldn't families be better off if they could get food assistance, immediately, with little hassle?

- Wouldn't access to health care be better if doctors were reimbursed faster, accurately, and with as little hassle as possible so they could spend more time with patients?

System of Work for Medicaid Reimbursement

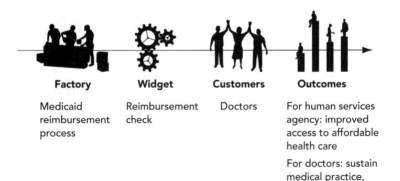

Factory	Widget	Customers	Outcomes
Medicaid reimbursement process	Reimbursement check	Doctors	For human services agency: improved access to affordable health care
			For doctors: sustain medical practice, serve more patients

System of Work for Foster Care Subsidies

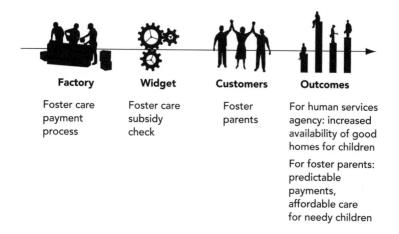

Factory	Widget	Customers	Outcomes
Foster care payment process	Foster care subsidy check	Foster parents	For human services agency: increased availability of good homes for children For foster parents: predictable payments, affordable care for needy children

System of Work for Food Stamp Distribution

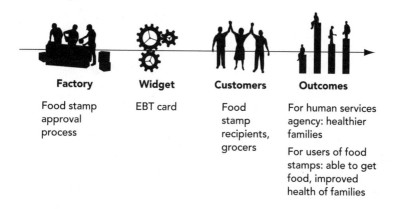

Factory	Widget	Customers	Outcomes
Food stamp approval process	EBT card	Food stamp recipients, grocers	For human services agency: healthier families For users of food stamps: able to get food, improved health of families

"We don't make widgets" is the excuse that allows us to ignore operations.

Imagine being the owner of a company and having the following conversation with your plant manager:

"How many widgets can you produce in a day?"
"A few. Some days more than others."
"Well how much do they cost to produce?"
"A little bit."
"How long would it take to get one?"
"A while."
"Well, are we making money?"
"That's a good question."

What would you do? Probably fire the manager on the spot. But isn't this exactly the way we answer these questions to elected officials? How much do things cost? We don't know, but we know how much we can spend. How long do things take? That depends. What results are we getting for our money? That's a good question.

Why are we unable to answer these most basic questions? Because we say we don't make widgets.

What Is a Widget, Exactly?

The key to improving government is to improve its factories (its systems). But it's hard to improve what we cannot see. A participant in one of my workshops best summarized the problem this way: Government is a bunch of hardworking people, trapped in dysfunctional systems, who produce invisible things for people who do not want them, on behalf of others who do, for reasons we rarely articulate and can hardly measure. I couldn't agree more.

The work of government is hard to get your arms around. It's often invisible—it's not made of sprockets, gears, or microchips. It's squishy and hard to define. And this is precisely what we have to change. It is the way we describe our work that is precisely what holds us back. We can't measure squishy. We can't manage squishy. But when we take squishy and make it into a tangible widget, we can begin to manage our systems like the best companies in the world and achieve greater results for citizens.

Robin Lawton offers a helpful definition.[1] A widget is something created by work, which can be given to someone else to achieve a desired outcome. What makes a widget a widget?

---

[1] The definition as well as the four rules (adapted) are from Robin L. Lawton, *Creating a Customer-Centered Culture: Leadership in Quality, Innovation, and Speed* (Milwaukee, Wis.: ASQC Quality Press, 1993), chap. 1, "The Service Product." www.imtC3.com.

1. **Widgets are things.** Cell phones, iPods, laptops, cars, TVs. These are all things. Helping, assisting, servicing, supporting, training, auditing, inspecting, leading—these are all activities. What's wrong with describing our work as activities? Activities are process, the "how" part of what we do. Customers don't care how we do what we do. Instead, they care about what we are going to give them to help them achieve their desired result. Defining our work in terms of things ensures we are not describing only activities.

Areas of Emphasis in the System of Work

Factory	Widget	Customers	Outcomes
How?	What?	Who?	Why?

2. **Widgets are deliverables.** You can deliver a widget to a customer. Many government managers will say that they produce knowledge or information. But those things don't magically appear. They are the outcome of a deliverable. When you read this book you receive knowledge (I hope). When you read an article you receive information. The books and the articles are the widgets. The easiest way

---

Two Kinds of Widgets

Just because we are trying to describe our squishy work more tangible—as widgets—doesn't mean a widget has to be physical. Widgets come in two types—those you can see coming out of a factory and loading on a truck (reports, permits, licenses, and so forth) and those that are invisible (answers, family meetings, facilitated sessions, assessments, and directions). Managers are more likely to produce the invisible kind.

As long as it meets the four rules, it's a widget.

to think of this is to imagine a large truck backing up to your cubicle. What would you load onto that truck? Those are your widgets. Auditing, inspecting, helping, serving, training, and supervising are not deliverables. They are the activities that produce the deliverables. The deliverables are the audit reports the customer receives, the notice of violation at the end of the inspection, the driver's license.

3. **Widgets can be counted.** Again, cell phones, iPods, laptops, cars, TVs. They all can be made plural with the addition of an s. You can envision shelves filled with them. Now try that with typical government employee responses to the what-do-you-do question. Protection(s). Economic development(s). Water(s). Law enforcement(s). Information(s). Because these activities are not countable, they are also not measurable.

4. **Widgets are specific.** An iPod, a cell phone, a Ford Mustang, a Rolex watch. When asked "what do you do?", most of us are more likely to recite a mission statement than articulate a specific widget.

We state a few broad things:

- create opportunity

- foster partnerships

- develop collaborations

- protect kids

- ensure health

- save the environment

Although these are lofty goals, they are of little help to us in actually improving the operations of the agency. These goals may describe the outcome of our work, but they don't get us any closer to finding the factories we need to improve to achieve those outcomes.

Perhaps another example will help. I was in a workshop with some Ob-Gyns from the U.S. Navy. When asked to define their widget, they immediately replied: babies. They were adamant about this, and what should have been a fifteen-minute exercise became an hour-and-a-half debate. The rule is: if anyone else can claim the widget as theirs, it is not ours. Might there be a couple of other people in the delivery room who would like to take credit for the baby?

What is really the widget of the Ob-Gyns? Deliveries. This is not just an issue of semantics. It gets to the heart of why so many of us in government struggle with improvement. The Ob-Gyns can't improve babies. They can improve their widgets (deliveries, prenatal examinations, instructions to the mother) in hopes of producing a healthy baby.

How do we get better results? Improve the widgets we produce:

- How do we get a cleaner environment? Improve our widgets (standards, permits, inspections, education sessions).

- How do we ensure health? Improve our widgets (restaurant inspections, epidemiology reports, vaccinations, insurance plans).

- How do we protect kids? Improve our widgets (child abuse investigation reports, foster home placements, summer job-training programs).

 BOX 3.2   **You Don't Make Money**

Many federal and state agencies like to say their widget is money. Unless they work in a treasury department, this is incorrect. The money is often an input that agencies manufacture into a grant.

The federal government passes grants on to its customers, the states, which repackage the grants and pass them on to their customers, the local agencies. Local agencies then create other widgets with the grant money. All along the way, widgets like regulations, contracts, performance standards, monitoring reports, and disbursements are being created.

In essence, we are trying to separate three concepts that consistently get muddled by our language—process, widget, outcome. Or, we are trying to separate the how from the what from the why. We do this because each needs to be measured, managed, and improved differently. Separating the concepts of process, widgets, and outcomes creates clarity and allows for better management, especially when we follow the four rules for defining our widgets: they are things, deliverable, countable, and specific (you can take credit for them).

 No Output

> You will also notice that we are not using the word *output*. This word has created much confusion for managers. Which is the output? The baby or the delivery? The permit or the reduced levels of particulate matter in the air? The child abuse investigation report or the safer kids?

Go ahead. Give it a try. Following these rules, identify the top five widgets your organization produces. Then identify the top five you personally produce. As you will see in the next chapter, the more specific your widget (a strategic plan, a wastewater permit, an expense account approval), the easier it will be to develop meaningful measures, improve customer satisfaction, and focus on outcomes.

I Object!

Congratulations! You are now a plant manager—responsible for quality, cost, speed, customer satisfaction, and results for your widgets. How's that feel? Here's the list of the usual objections I get to this concept:

- **This is small thinking.** We're not here to produce reports and plans. We're here to make lives better for citizens. Absolutely true. Unfortunately, the only methods we have to make lives

Worksheet for Identifying Widgets

Five widgets my organization produces:

-
-
-
-
-

Five widgets I personally produce:

-
-
-
-
-

better for citizens is through the widgets we produce. Results don't materialize out of thin air. They are the outcomes obtained when customers use the things we produce. If you want better results (outcomes), your options are actually very few: change what you produce (the widget), or change how you produce it (the process).

- **This doesn't accurately reflect what I really do.** No, it only makes visible the means by which you do what you do. You may be in charge of "changing the culture," but that only happens through the widgets you create and deliver to customers—things like strategic plans, focus groups, employee forums, counseling sessions, and change management workshops.

- **My widget is service.** What is service? This is perhaps one of the least helpful words in our vocabulary. Service is a broad, fuzzy, intangible word that brings us no closer to being able to measure, manage, or improve what we do. We might as well say my widget is "stuff," a term that would be just as useful. Often what we

Agencies, Agency Functions, and the Widgets They Produce

Kinds of agencies	Typical widgets
Environmental	Permits, notices of violation, rules, and regulations
Parks and recreation	Parks, events (county fairs, tournaments), acres of maintained land
Public works	Sewer connections, gallons of water
Transportation	Miles of roads, filled potholes, bus lines
Economic development	Tax credits, company relocation proposals, community development grants
Labor	Unemployment checks, job matches, workers' compensation appeal decisions
Corrections	Inmate cells, GED programs, victims' compensation funds
Revenue	Tax returns, collections cases, refunds, disbursements
DMVs	Driver's licenses, car titles, license plates
Health	Vaccinations, restaurant inspection reports, epidemiology reports
Collections	Tax rolls, appeals decisions
Probation and parole	Parole decisions, probation visits, revocations
Public defenders	Defense cases
Professional registration	Licenses, revocations, suspensions
Mental health	Treatment plans, supervised activities, respite care hours
Social services	Child abuse investigation reports, food stamps, Medicaid reimbursements, job-training classes, foster home licenses

Kinds of functions	Typical widgets
Information technology	Networks, PC repairs, installations, applications
Human resources	Filled vacancies, policies, training classes, new-employee orientation
Purchasing	Approved purchase orders, contracts, requests for proposals, vendor lists
Budget analysts	Budget recommendations
Managers	Plans, procedures, performance appraisals, coaching sessions, answers, assignments, approvals

mean by service is "helping"—an activity. The widget behind "helping" is often "answers." Most of us are in the answer business. We can count how many answers we produce, how long they take to produce, what percentage are correct, and how happy customers are with them. Some answers are reactive (after the question), and others are proactive. Isn't a budget document really a proactive, prepackaged answer to the questions, How much do you plan on spending? On what things? Isn't a day-care license a prepackaged answer to the question, Is this a safe place to leave my child?

- **My widget is a motivated staff.** Please see the earlier discussion regarding babies. Can I buy a motivated staff from you? How much does one cost? How long does it take you to make one? Do they come in green? Again, a motivated staff is the outcome obtained when customers use your widgets—feedback sessions, training programs, pats on the back, challenging assignments. (And you can't motivate people anyway.)

- **I don't have any widgets.** I hope that isn't true. If you don't produce anything, might I suggest you start producing a new widget—a résumé. Everyone has widgets. Keep looking. What do you deliver to your customers?

Governments produce hundreds if not thousands of widgets. We're a lot more complicated than Ford. Actually, Ford produces thousands of widgets as well, all culminating in, say, a Mustang. The Mustang is the big widget we see at the end of the big factory. But if you trace back to the beginning, you will see hundreds of little factories producing widgets like market analysis, product concepts, product designs, budgets, specifications, supplier contracts, production schedules, and on and on. This chain of widgets leads to the big widget.

Your agency is quite similar. Offices such as legal, accounting, human resources, IT, policy, and many other areas produce widgets in the horizontal chains that produce your big widgets. (Law leads to regulations, regulations lead to policies, and policies lead to standards, all leading to the widget we deliver to the customer.) Most government agencies have very few Mustangs, but they have lots of "component parts" that go into the Mustangs.

BOX 3.4   Who Thinks They Don't Make Widgets?

The argument, "We don't make widgets," actually applies to just about everybody now. Only 14 percent of American workers (who don't work on farms) are actively engaged in manufacturing widgets, and this percentage is dropping daily. Even inside a typical manufacturing organization, fewer than 15 percent of the employees are making the widgets.

What's everybody else doing? Look back at your list. We're all in the same boat. The lessons of this book apply not just to government but to about 86 percent of the workforce.

"Oh, this is just semantics." Please remember you said this after you read the next chapter.

So, if you're a plant manger, I guess we should talk about what plant managers do. Again, these concepts are rarely taught to government managers, and when they are, they usually get lost in translation because "we don't make widgets."

System of Work and Plant Managers' Tasks

Factory	Widget	Customers	Outcomes
1. Work with suppliers	2. Reengineering 3. Quality control	4. Customer satisfaction	5. Innovation

Plant managers improve by having sophisticated initiati around each interaction in the system-of-work model:

1. Plant managers work with suppliers to ensure inputs into the process are of the highest quality. This spawned initiatives like just-in-time inventory, ISO 9000, and supply-chain management.

2. Plant managers reengineer their processes to drive out as much wasted time and resources as possible. From this, we have initiatives like lean manufacturing, reengineering, and the theory of constraints.

3. Plant managers work to ensure that each widget comes off the line 100 percent perfect the first time. This gave us the original Total Quality Management (TQM) movement, which has morphed into Six Sigma.

4. Plant managers work proactively with customers to design products that meet their expectations. Initiatives in this area include quality function deployment, the voice of the customer, and myriad service and satisfaction initiatives.

5. Plant managers use outcome-focused innovation to develop entirely new products to better achieve results for customers and the organization. The field of innovation is an emerging one, and the science is just now coming in on what works. The implications to business are enormous but are nothing in comparison with how they can be applied in government (this will be the focus of chapter 5).

Imagine what would happen if government could do these things, too? We can, and finding your widgets is the first key step.

Measurement Made Easy

To manage the plant, we have to understand the plant. And measurement is how we arrive at understanding. I understand that asking many government managers to measure things is akin to asking a child to eat more broccoli. Yet measurement is important:

eveal our values. If we value customer satisfaction, e it. If we care about speed, we'll measure it. You can vhat is important to an organization by looking at ures. I was working with a government call center ..ggling with customer satisfaction, employee morale, and an ever-increasing call volume. When I asked to see the measures that supervisors used to run the place, I was shocked to see only two: how many calls each employee handled during an hour and how long each employee was taking to finish a call. What values were these measures reinforcing? Mush! Did the organization care about whether the customers were receiving the right answers, and whether they got all their questions answered on the first call? No. Their measures were perfectly suited for the sweatshop they had created.

- **Measures drive behavior.** Given the measures in the above call center, it was no surprise to see how the employees behaved. Many employees would answer a call and immediately hang up or pass it on to the next level, giving themselves short talk times and many calls answered. Few would go the extra mile to fully understand customer questions because they had to get off the phone. If measures drive behavior, then we need to be sure that we are measuring the right things. If we want to be faster, we should measure process speed. If we want to be more customer focused, we should measure customer satisfaction.

- **Measures can inspire us.** 61* home runs, the United Way campaign thermometer you pass on the way to work, the pounds I see I've shed when I get on the scale—they all inspire us. One of the top motivators for employees is the feeling that they are making a difference. Measurement helps them see that. Imagine playing basketball eight hours a day every day and not keeping score. After a while, it would get a little boring. Unfortunately, most employees live like this. Am I winning? Are we getting better? Are we making a difference? Measurement helps us see that.

- **And, most important, measures help us learn.** This is the true purpose: to help us answer important questions. How long does this take? Is it working? Are we having an impact? What happened? As long as these questions don't start with "who," they can transform the intelligence of the organization.

BOX 3.5 How to Drive Your Staff Crazy— Example 2

A useful customer satisfaction measure for DMV offices is how long customers wait in line.

In one state, each month the managers of the various DMV offices assembled to share results of their wait-time calculations. What they always found was that customers waited longer in some offices than others, some offices improved, and others didn't. At the end of each manager's presentation, the administrator would start by asking "why?" "Why did they wait twenty minutes this month compared with eighteen minutes last month? Why did they wait ten minutes this month compared with fifteen minutes last month?"

Of course, no manager wants to answer, "I don't know," so they came up with reasons. "Marge was out sick for a week." "We worked real hard this month." "I made cookies for the staff." The more times they were asked, the more reasons they made up. Why were they making things up? Not because they didn't know the reasons for the variance in performance, but because there weren't any reasons for the variance in performance.

One of the great tragedies of TQM's failure in government was that we missed one of its greatest teachings—the understanding of variance. The performance of any process will vary around its mean. Another way of saying this is that what goes up must come down—then it goes back up again, and then down again for a little while, and then up again, and on and on. Why? Because of countless reasons inside the system.

What are all the reasons that the wait times can vary in a DMV? The weather, the number of people who show up at exactly the same time, the number of days in the month, and the complexity of the transactions. All of these little things are happening all the time. This is called common-

continued

BOX 3.5

How to Drive Your Staff Crazy—Example 2 *continued*

cause variation. At the DMVs in this particular state, wait times fluctuated between ten minutes and thirty-five minutes, with a mean of close to fifteen minutes. If performance was anywhere between ten and thirty-five minutes, there really was no point in asking why. The system was just as likely to produce a twenty-eight-minute wait time as a twelve-minute wait time. If, however, the wait times are at forty-five minutes or at eight minutes, we should repeatedly ask why until we find the culprit. This is called special-cause variation. That is, the cause of the performance is outside the system. Something happened that wasn't supposed to.

Why does this matter? Because we tend to look for special causes in a common-cause world. We send our staffs on wild-goose chases to find reasons where there are none. To make things worse, we treat common causes like special causes. We reward a manager when performance goes up, and then we question our judgment when performance goes down the next month.

A system is finely tuned to deliver exactly the results that it is achieving. If you want different results, you have to change the system.

Why, then, is meaningful measurement like pulling teeth? One of my workshop participants answered this best when he said: "Why would I build you the club you are going to use to hit me on the head?" People don't want to measure because measures are used for either the wrong purpose—"blamestorming"—or for no purpose at all. Would you do something that was hard work, that could get you in trouble even if done well, and that rarely led to pleasure?

But it doesn't have to be this way. The best way to get meaningful measures is not to ask for measures, but to ask for answers—answers to questions that everyone wants to know. People have an intrinsic thirst for knowledge, and most have a strong desire to be right. An unanswered question is often enough to unleash the researcher in all of us.

To manage the plant, we've got to measure the plant. The key to measuring the plant is asking questions. What are the right questions?

- How many of these widgets are we able to produce?
- How many of these widgets do we need to produce?
- How long does it take to make the widget?
- How much does it cost to make the widget?
- What percentage of the widgets makes it through the factory correctly on the first try?
- How much does it cost us and our customers when there are mistakes?
- What do customers want from this widget?
- Are the customers getting what they want?
- What results are we hoping to achieve with this widget?
- Are we achieving those results?

Having said all that, let me add this quote from Peter Block: "[A]ggressive measuring changes the learning and behavior of a human being to the same extent that meteorology can change the weather."[2]

Doesn't this contradict everything I just said? Nope. It reinforces it.

Measurement exists to start the conversation. Without action, the conversation is meaningless. To paraphrase Peter Scholtes: measuring systems doesn't improve systems, talking about systems doesn't improve systems, improving systems improves systems. A system is

---

[2] Peter Block, "Someone to Watch Over Me," *News for a Change*, March 2001.

finely tuned to provide you with the exact results you are currently getting. Stretch targets don't change the system. Incentives don't change the system. If you want a different result, you have to change the system. What can we change? The components of the system-of-work model. We can:

- change *how* we do what we do by improving the process, or
- change *what* we do by building widgets that better satisfy customers, or
- develop completely new widgets that better achieve organizational and customer-desired outcomes.

Items two and three will be handled in subsequent chapters. The remainder of this chapter will focus on item one—improving the factories that make the widgets.

Fast Government

I had the grave misfortune of working in government at the height of the TQM fad. The agency I worked for brought in some of the leading quality gurus from manufacturing, who set about dazzling us with control charts and visions of a defect-free world. If only we could have better grasped the fine points of the Pareto chart, we could have revived our state's lagging economy. Of course none of the people in the room thought they made widgets, and the concepts of statistical process control didn't set their hearts on fire. The whole effort got lost in translation.

Speaking of lost in translation—at one point, with this same agency, we had the opportunity to meet Dr. Genichi Taguchi, who is from Japan and is an absolute legend in the field of quality improvement. Even though the TQM stuff wasn't making a lot of sense to our agency, we still awaited his wisdom with great anticipation. There was just one problem—he didn't speak English ... at all. At the end of a very frustrating day (for all of us—we couldn't understand his language much less his theories, and he couldn't understand why we didn't see that quality principles applied to government), our liaison offered Dr. Taguchi the chance to make a parting shot. He asked him, "Dr. Taguchi, given all of your knowledge of quality and what you've learned today about American government agencies, what is the one thing these government managers should focus on to improve?" After a lengthy pause, Dr. Taguchi uttered his only two words of English that day: "Maybe speed?"

My colleagues and I laughed about that day for years until we were in a position to lead an organization, and then it hit us: the good doctor was right. It is all about speed. To improve government factories, we have to make them run faster, and, by doing so, we will decrease costs and increase quality.

I should have cautioned you that when you realize that your agency is full of factories, you may not want to look too closely. Our factories get pretty messed up. They are often slow, cumbersome, complex, error riddled, and full of exception routes. Right next to the factory is usually someone scurrying around putting out fires all day long. Why do our government factories get so messed up? They usually don't start that way. What starts out as a simple task—perhaps licensing a nurse or issuing a building permit—becomes a seventy-five-step nightmare as the following takes place:

1. The organizational structure changes.

2. Mistakes happen, which leads to the creation of new steps to ensure these mistakes never happen again. (The DNA of most processes is usually CYA.)

3. Turnover increases.

4. Micromanagers enter the picture.

5. Computer systems are modified or added.

6. Legislation is passed.

7. Auditors introduce more controls.

8. Special-interest groups emerge.

9. The boss says so.

10. Legal counsel wants to minimize risks.

Behind most of these is the desire for control.

A typical scenario goes something like this: A permit factory cuts across three organizational silos. Things go fine for awhile, as permit applications go from silo A to B to C with few problems. Then one gets lost. Silo C blames silo B, which blames silo A. A's manager gets chewed out by the big boss. Using the keen survival skills that earned her this job in the first place, A's manager sets about to make sure this never happens again. She creates a new policy that nothing goes to silo B without being checked and double-checked. To manage the double-checking, all applications will be grouped in batches of 100. A signed cover sheet will be attached to the batch so we know who to blame if something goes wrong again. Silo A's manager just CYA'd A. Of course the manager of silo B is pretty sharp as well. There is no way he's going to take A's word for it that all 100 items are actually in the batch and have been handled correctly. So B institutes a policy that all batches received from A will be counted, recounted, and verified for accuracy. At the end of this inspection, a new cover sheet will be affixed bearing the signature of someone from silo B so we know who to blame if something goes wrong.

Ahhh, sweet complexity, and this was with only two handoffs. Most government factories have about ten. To paraphrase that ancient mystic, Master Yoda: mistakes lead to blame. Blame leads to CYA. CYA leads to the dark side.

From this example you can see how I can boldly and confidently insist that every significant government factory can run 80 percent faster. Yes, 80 percent. I have yet to work with a team that missed this target. How can I be so sure? It's easy when you understand Einstein's theory of relativity as it applies to most people every day: The length of a minute is relative, depending on which side of the bathroom door you are on.

In any given factory, there are two kinds of time occurring:

- Work time: time during a process when actual work is happening

- Elapsed time: the total time the process takes (work time plus any time spent on handoffs, waiting, batches, backlog, and so on)

Another way to think about it: Work time is what the guy who finished your basement billed you for. Elapsed time was how long your lives were completely disrupted before that @#$*% guy actually finished the job. (Sorry, posttraumatic stress disorder.)

What's the difference between the two? Between 95 and 99.5 percent.[3] That is, at least 95 percent of all time in a process is waste. Think about it. How long does it take you to get your expense account reimbursed? About 30 days? Do you honestly believe that there is a group of employees toiling away in a sweatshop for 30 straight days to forge the perfect check? Of that 30 days, how much actual work time is there? About 5 minutes. Where does all the time go?

- in-baskets and out-baskets

- waiting for signatures

- inspections and reinspections

- waiting for enough expense accounts to make a batch

- waiting for the computer system to run

- conforming to a policy that says we only process expense accounts once a month

Wouldn't it be nice to get reimbursed five minutes after your trip? That is what a good plant manager does—strips away all the things that add time and complexity to the factory.

Focusing on either unit of time—elapsed time or work time—yields different results.

When we close the gap between elapsed time and work time, we're faster, more responsive, and more flexible. We give the customer what the customer wants when the customer wants it. We also inevitably cut out unnecessary tasks (the batching, rebatching, inspecting, and reinspecting), which frees up staff time to do other value-added tasks.

When we cut work time, we save money. For example, if we cut the work time to process an application from ten minutes to five minutes, we've saved five minutes of work. If we process seventy-five a day, we just freed up a full-time employee. It is important to stress that it is entirely possible to cut work time in one area and still

---

[3] George Stalk Jr. and Thomas M. Hout *Competing against Time: How Time-Based Competition Is Reshaping Global Markets* (New York: Free Press, 1990).

have the process take just as long. For example, we may save five minutes of work time in Unit A, but Unit B may still process applications only on Mondays.

One of my favorite change projects was trying to reform a tax-refund factory. The project was chosen because it would have a noticeable impact on citizens. I started the project on April 15th (could there be a better day?) with a guided tour of the factory. At every station (there were fourteen separate ones—one to open the envelopes, another to take the items out of the envelopes, another to remove the staples, another to restaple, and on and on), I asked the workers two questions: How long does it take you to do this? (this is the work time), and How much time usually passes from the time you get it until it goes on to the next station? (the elapsed time). At the end of the tour I knew two undeniable facts:

- The process took at least twenty-seven days from the time a tax return was received until the taxpayer received a check.

- During that twenty-seven days, three minutes of actual work were performed.

Where did those tax returns spend all that time?

- in-baskets and out-baskets

- sitting in piles of backlog

- inspections and reinspections

- waiting for enough returns to make a batch

- waiting for the computer system to run

- caught in an outdated and misguided policy that says we only process refunds on weekends (behind every process problem is usually a policy problem)

Wouldn't it be nice to get your tax refund three minutes after you filed it? My group got close. With the ingenuity of some amazing staff, we were able to get the refunds out of our factory in three days. A 90 percent improvement in time. And we did it at lower cost. By fixing the batches, backlogs, and bottlenecks, we freed up resources. By trimming the work time from three minutes per refund to two and a half minutes, we freed up more than 40 employees to be used elsewhere. And the customers, of course, loved it.

One of the most common factories in government is the permit factory. The permit widget gets cranked out at the federal, state, county, and city levels. And no factory is as cursed as the permit factory. I was asked to help with an environmental permitting factory that was about to be pillaged and burned to the ground by its customers. (The question of "who is the customer" in a regulatory environment is a complex issue and one we will address in the next chapter.) Of course, the first step was to figure out how well the factory was performing. So I asked the basic questions:

Me: How long does it take to process one of the permit applications?
Them: The statutes say we have 90 days.
Me: Yes, but how long does it actually take?
Them: Once everything is correct, 90 days.
Me: Well, how many come in correct the first time?
Them: None.
Me: How long does it take them to get it right?
Them: A few months. They usually end up hiring a consultant to meet all the requirements.
Me: What happens to their development project while all this is going on?
Them: No development.
Me: How much does that cost them?
Them: The cost of the permit is $250.
Me: No, how much does the whole process—including hiring the consultant and the months they lose on their development—cost them?
(Sounds of crickets chirping.)

Measures reveal our values. What values did these measures reveal? We're not in any hurry, we don't care that you can't operate, it's not our fault you can't fill out the form correctly—essentially that you, the customer, are here to serve us.

We also experienced the gravitational pull of legislative standards. Parkinson's law states that work will expand to fill the amount of

Myth 1: We Don't Make Widgets

Why it matters:

- To improve an organization, you have to improve its systems (the processes that produce widgets for customers to achieve results).

- The squishy way we describe our work in government makes it difficult to see the systems, making it hard to measure, manage, and improve (which leads to the crazy ways we try to make changes).

- When we finally see the widgets, we become like plant managers and can use all the tools they have at their disposal to make the widgets better and the government factories more efficient. And why do we want to do this? So we can better satisfy customers and achieve a higher return for our investors.

- Widgets are the connection between what we care about and manage (our activities), our customers, and results. When we can't see the widget, we focus our attention on how we do things, and we forget about who we do them for and why.

The truth:

We do make widgets—the tangible deliverables produced in our government factories that we deliver to customers in order to achieve results. It is our responsibility to achieve a higher return for investors by making these widgets better, faster, and cheaper.

time allotted for it. Eli Goldratt calls this the "student syndrome."[4] If a teacher allows two weeks to write a report, it will take two weeks. If a student has two days, it will take two days. This same effect takes place in a government factory. It's amazing, but we can take a gov-

---

[4] Eliyau M. Goldratt, *Critical Chain* (Great Barrington, Mass.: North River Press, 1997).

What to measure:

- How many widgets we produce
- How long it takes to produce a widget
- How long it takes a customer to get a widget
- How much it costs to make a widget
- How many widgets are produced correctly on the first try
- How satisfied customers are with the widget
- What results the widget is achieving

How to improve:

- Talk with customers to determine their expectations for the widget (the subject of the next chapter).

- Design the widget to meet customers' expectations.

- Create a flowchart for the existing process that produces the widget.

- Calculate the two units of time: elapsed time and work time.

- Close the gap between elapsed time and work time by at least 80 percent by eliminating handoffs, cutting batches and batch sizes, eliminating bottlenecks, processing in parallel, and reducing inspections.

- Identify ways to reduce the work time.

- Use problem solving to reduce errors and variance in the process.

- Involve employees in the improvement process.

ernment factory that produces widgets every ten days, create a legislative standard that says they can take no longer than thirty days, and, with no change in staffing, the factory will miraculously start turning out widgets every thirty days. Beware of standards!

There is not enough space here to teach everything you need to know to make your factories run 80 percent faster. For more specific methods and tools, I encourage you to read chapter 4 of my earlier book, *The Change Agent's Guide to Radical Improvement* (ASQ Quality Press). Government factories big and small have used the concepts to build their widgets better, faster, and cheaper.

The Factory between Your Ears

For many of us, our factory is between our ears; that is, we don't amass large quantities of the same widgets—forms or tax returns or permits. Instead, we continually have to create new, customized widgets—for example, a legal opinion, a project plan, a management decision. This is the nature of what Peter Drucker termed "knowledge work."[5] The essence of knowledge work, as Drucker noted, is that work has to be defined before it can be produced. For knowledge workers—and nearly all managers and professionals are knowledge workers—the critical skill is not to just crank out widgets but to know which widgets to crank out. Essential for this task is the ability to understand what customers want and deliver it correctly the first time. How to do this is covered in the next chapter.

---

[5] Peter F. Drucker, *The Essential Drucker: The Best of Sixty Years of Peter Drucker's Essential Writings on Management* (New York: Collins, 2003).

Chapter  4

We Don't Have Customers

How would you manage differently if your survival depended on customer satisfaction?

We've come a long way in government with respect to the concept of customers. I led a planning retreat for a federal job-training agency in the early 1990s that got quite heated after I had the audacity to suggest they might want to work with their customers to find out what the customers wanted from the agency.

One gentleman in particular started ranting and raving about how "we're government and we don't have customers." Other people stepped in to argue with him in my defense. The debate got so intense that I had to call a time-out and separate the parties. In the hallway, I got Mr. We-Don't-Have-Customers to calm down and acquiesce for the sake of argument that maybe the agency had some customers. Then, being the good troublemaker that I am, I pulled them all back together and said, "Now that we all agree we have customers, let's get clear on who they are." This one nearly came to blows: The customer was the job seeker; no, it was the employer; no, it was society as a whole; and on and on.

Fortunately the state of thinking has progressed past this point, and we are no longer arguing over whether we have customers and whether we should satisfy them. Instead, government managers are trying to figure out how to satisfy our customers, given our unique constraints.

The debate has moved from "Why do this?" to "How do we do this?"

Having said that, let's delve into "Why do this." Why does customer satisfaction matter in government? After all, we really don't have customers, we have hostages. They didn't choose us, they don't want to be with us, and given a choice they wouldn't come back. Recall the quote from the introductory chapter: "Government is a bunch of hardworking people, trapped in dysfunctional systems, who produce invisible things for people who do not want them, on behalf of others who do want these things for reasons we rarely articulate and can hardly measure."

Why bother? Some try to use the threat that if we don't do better for our customers, we will go out of business or get privatized. I have never found this argument to be very believable or particularly useful. We don't need to scare employees into caring about customers. We need to appeal to their natural, intrinsic desire to be excellent and to help people. We are, after all, public servants. We don't come to work for government to get rich. We come to serve. And that is why customer satisfaction matters—it is our very reason for being. Our customers are often the neediest people in society— the poor, the unemployed, the mentally and physically ill. How is it that BMW cares more about the yuppie buying his third Beemer than we do about our customers? We live to serve, and we should do it spectacularly.

Another reason why customer satisfaction in government matters can best be understood if we talk about the uncontroversial topics of religion and money. George Carlin's famous line is that there are only two things he knows about God: he isn't Him, and that He is always short of cash. This is a commonly held belief about religion and tithing. All the world's religions ask their followers to give them money—not because the religious group is short of cash, but for what it does for the giver. Giving helps the giver as much as the receiver. It changes the heart. We give to the church not because they need it but because we need it.

The same is true about customer satisfaction in government. We focus on it because it changes the hearts of the people who work in the agency. It allows them to serve and lets them make a difference in people's lives. Have you ever experienced a culture where everyone was focused on helping and serving others? Contrast that with a culture where everyone is focused on helping and serving themselves. I'd prefer to work in the former.

The final reason why customer satisfaction matters in government is a very practical one. You'll recall from the previous chapter the point that widgets are the only means by which we achieve our outcomes. That is, all of our policies, plans, and strategies (a.k.a. talk) manifest themselves and become tangible only through the widgets we produce in our factories. It is by the customers using the widgets we have created for them that we achieve our desired results. If we create a widget that customers don't like and can't use, we will struggle to achieve our results.

 BOX 4.1   Goal Congruence

One of the nice things about government is that our desired outcomes are often the same as what our customers want. An unemployed person wants to find a high-wage job, and we also want them to. A mother wants her child to stay well, and we do, too. This goal congruence is often not the case in the private sector.

For example, one of the ways we try to produce a better environment is to issue permits that constrain the amount of pollution a company may create. The permit is the widget. As we discuss later in this chapter, that permit may have multiple customers, but there are definitely two we can identify right away—the plant manager and the environmental agency inspector. Both individuals rely on the permit to determine how and whether the plant is in compliance. In customer research I conducted with a team on this project, it was amazing what we learned: neither the plant managers nor the inspectors could make any sense of the permit. Both sides were guessing about whether they were in compliance and what the agency wanted them to do. All the laws, regulations, policies, and good intentions about a clean environment and corporate responsibility manifested themselves in one widget—the permit—and that widget was completely unable to perform its duty. If the customer can't use the widget, we can't achieve our outcomes.

The Word *Customer*

So why do we struggle so much with the concept of customer? So much so that we're afraid to say the word out loud. I was testifying in a state senate appropriations hearing about some radical changes that we were making, and I was running down the list of cost savings and improvements we'd made for customers when the chair of the committee interrupted and said, "Son, if you use the word 'customer' in my chambers again I will have you escorted out. We are government. We don't have customers." Although I quickly shut up about customers, every ounce of me wanted to drive him to the family support offices and show him the lines of "not customers" that stretched around the block.

Over time, agencies have come up with numerous other terms to avoid using the dreaded word, *customer:*

- applicant
- attendee
- candidate
- case
- citizen
- claimant
- client
- complier
- defendant
- driver
- family
- inmate
- job seeker
- offender
- parolee
- permitee
- recipient
- requestor
- resident
- violator

Why can't we just say *customer*? Because there is so much baggage associated with that word. When we think of customers in the traditional sense, we think of someone who is going to buy something and use it. That just doesn't hold up in government.

Who Is the Customer?

We struggle with the concept of customer for three main reasons:

1. We Talk about Customers in the Abstract

Most who-is-the-customer fights occur because we talk about customers in broad generalities. For example environmental agencies get really upset if you say that their customers are industry. Correctional agencies get upset if you tell them that inmates are their customers. Tax auditors will pummel you if you say that tax cheats are their customers. And the staff in these agencies are justified in being upset. In the abstract, these statements make them uncomfortable. Environmental agencies are here to protect the environment, not cater to industry. Corrections officers are here to protect the public, not coddle inmates. Tax auditors are here to find tax cheaters and bring them to justice. So, these can't be their customers. Except they are.

The problem is that we are talking about these customers in the abstract—that is, independent of any specific widget. Let's try it again with some widgets:

- Who is the customer for an environmental regulation, an appeal hearing, a compliance workshop, or a permit application form? Industry.

- Who is the customer for a prison meal, a general equivalency diploma (GED) program, and an offender job placement program? Inmates.

- Who is the customer for tax regulations, an audit report, an appeal hearing, and a payment plan? Tax cheats.

Government gets in fights about who is the customer because we speak in broad terms and generalities. This is fine for your mission statement, but it doesn't help manage the operations. Any discussion of who is the customer must be preceded by a clear definition of which widget we are talking about. Who is the customer for what? The answer will change every time the widget changes. You see now why we spent so much time in the previous chapter talking about widgets. Identifying the exact widget not only is the key to unlocking our potential to be better, faster, and cheaper, but it also forever ends the debate about customers.

BOX 4.2 — And You Are ... ?

The staff of a state labor department created a classic example of government's confusion about customers. Thinking about customers in the abstract—and wrongly surmising that taxpayers are the customers—they decided to carry out a customer satisfaction survey. This well-crafted instrument was sent to thousands upon thousands of citizens of the state, and it asked such questions as "How satisfied are you with the labor department?" "Please rate the labor department on the following things ... " The return rate was only 7 percent, and what did the citizens say? "Who in the @#$% is the labor department?"

A far more useful exercise would have been to talk to the actual customers for the labor department's widgets— unemployed people who used the department's checks and job-matching resources and employers who used the department's workers' compensation appeal process and job placement resources.

Let me offer a real-life example of the consequences of defining customers in the abstract. I was working with staff who were in charge of a child abuse investigation factory. When you asked them who their customers were, they of course gave the mission statement answer: the kids. That's fine; they are there to protect kids. So I then asked them how the kids liked the child abuse investigation reports (their widget). They said the kids never read them. "Exactly," I responded. So who is the customer of the child abuse investigation report? Again they said "kids." So I asked again which parts of the report the kids have enjoyed most. Finally the light bulbs went on. Who uses the report? Prosecutors. Prosecutors are the customers for their widget. Because they did not understand this and did not think of prosecutors as their customers (all along they had thought their customers were always the kids), they had never talked to prosecutors about how they liked the widget. It turned out the prosecutors hated the widget. Prosecutors thought the reports were indecipherable, inconsistent, lacking critical facts, and often unsupportable in court. Other than that, they were fine.

Again, consequences of the myths are real. The way we achieve our outcomes is by customers using our widgets successfully. The mission to protect kids was made manifest in the widget—child abuse investigation reports. If the customer could not successfully use the widget, then the outcomes could not be obtained. How can kids be better protected? Build a better widget (the child abuse investigation report) that the customers (the prosecutors) can use to put away the bad people.

The legal profession has taught us many things over the years, but perhaps nothing has been as helpful as lawyers' standard industry response to any question: "It depends." Ask any attorney a question, and the first answer you'll hear is "It depends." We should follow their lead anytime someone asks who the customer is: "It depends. Which widget are you talking about?"

2. We Think Taxpayers Are the Customers

What could possibly be wrong with that? Please reread the paragraphs above. Are taxpayers the customers? It depends. Which widget are we talking about?

To say that our customers are the taxpayers is the equivalent of Ford saying its customers are their shareholders and investors. That's crazy talk (most of them drive Mercedes). The following model presents a framework for thinking about government that again shatters some critical myths and allows us to see that we are in fact a lot more like our private-sector counterparts than we are different.

In a typical company, you have investors. They invest in the company in hopes of achieving a return (in the private sector that return is measured in dollars). These investors get together and elect a board of directors to oversee the company and ensure that the investment they are making achieves the highest possible return. This board of directors in turn hires a CEO to run the organization. Under the CEO are a series of business units all cranking out widgets that are pur-

BOX 4.3 Words That Confuse

One prominent author in the field of improving government further confuses the who-is-the-customer issue by introducing new terms like *compliers* (people who have to pay speeding tickets, for example). What good does this distinction do? Do we now have the right to flog compliers because they are not customers? Shouldn't we treat a speeder like a customer? Isn't each speeder the customer for the ticket (each ticket should clearly indicate what the speeder did wrong, what is owed, and how the obligation can be fulfilled), for the court date (shouldn't the speeder have some choice?), for the speed limit signs, and for the payment process?

When we talk about customers in the abstract, independent of a specific widget, we have fights. New terms like compliers don't help. Neither do terms like *stakeholders* (What are they holding? If it's not the widget, then they are not the customer.) or *internal customers* vs. *external customers* (What do internal and external tell us other than where they physically reside?).

Parallels between Government and Private Business

	Business	Government
▲	Investors	Taxpayers
Accountability	Board of directors	Government board or legislature
	CEO	County manager or state governor
	Business unit	Department or division
	Products or services	Products or services

chased by customers so that the investors can achieve their return. Are Ford's investors their customers? No, they are their investors. When would they be customers? When they buy a Ford car.

The same model applies to government. (We will go into more detail on this in the next chapter.) Let's take a typical county government. The county government has investors called taxpayers. Now, granted, they are investing involuntarily, but the analogy holds. These taxpayers are investing in the county for what reason? They want a return, only their return is not measured in dollars. Profit margin is measured in jobs created, less traffic congestion, fewer illnesses, greater appreciation of the natural resources, and a higher quality of life. Like all investors, they want more of this return for less money. These investors get together and elect a board of directors to oversee the company (in some counties these are called a board of supervisors) and ensure that the investment they are making achieves the highest possible return. This board in turn hires a CEO (the county manager) to run the organization. Under the CEO are a series of business units (often called divisions and departments and, under them, smaller units often called programs) all cranking out widgets for customers so that the investors can achieve their return. Are the taxpayers the customers? No, they are the investors. When would they be customers? When they use any of the widgets that the county produces—a park, a building permit, the county fair, a flu vaccination.

I hope you see the parallel because this concept has confused and confounded government managers forever. And how can it not be confusing? Taxpayers themselves are confused. In one breath they are yelling at us that they demand to be treated like customers and in the next breath they tell us that they pay our salaries. Which is it? Calling taxpayers customers demeans their role. The taxpayers own the company. They are the investors and should be treated accordingly. The next chapter will go into depth about what that means. Are taxpayers also customers? It depends. Which widget are you talking about?

3. We Have Multiple Customers, Often with Competing Interests
I can sympathize with this because this is perhaps one of the hardest things about managing in government—but that's why you get paid the big bucks!

Yes, customer satisfaction would be easy if we in government had only one customer, but that's not our reality. This is of course nobody's reality—companies have to satisfy multiple customers with competing interests as well. A tube of toothpaste should be easy to open, not messy, and taste good. It also has to fit neatly into the space Wal-Mart has allotted for it; comply with the distribution, bar coding, and return requirements Wal-Mart has; meet FDA requirements; and be approved by four out of five dentists. And Boeing could easily build an amazingly comfortable airplane that would allow all of us to have endless amounts of leg room and storage, but those pesky airlines have other priorities.

The problem in government is that we tend to lump these multiple customers with competing interests into only one group and call them customers (if we in government are even allowed to use that word). This can have grave consequences.

One of my favorite projects was an initiative to improve tax forms, mainly because I couldn't figure them out and I wanted revenge. When I train change agents, I always share this maxim: Any project you are about to embark on has already been tried at least five times. Go find the old binders.

As I dug through the old binders of the past tax form improvement teams, a funny thing emerged. Somewhere around the third or fourth initiative, they decided it might be nice to get customer input. So a list was made of all the customers for the tax form, including taxpayers, tax preparers and certified public accountants (CPAs), the Internal Revenue Service (IRS), internal processing staff, auditors, and others. As they reviewed the list, they decided that taxpayers would be too hard to track down and might be intimidated. So they settled on some of the other groups, mainly the tax preparers. Any problem with that? Well, as a taxpayer, what is the number one expectation you have for a tax form? That it be simple. But what is the number one expectation of tax preparers? Complex. Uh-oh. The more input the agency got from tax preparers, the more complex the forms got. (An interesting sidebar: Congress passed legislation banning the IRS from building any product that would allow taxpayers to do their taxes easily online, for fear that it might hurt CPAs and software companies. After all, they are customers, too. Right?) This is what happens when we fail to differentiate customers by their roles.

Understanding that customers are defined by the widget is half the battle. The other half is just as important: understanding that customers can play different roles with that widget. Yes, taxpayers, tax preparers, and TurboTax are all customers of tax forms, but one of them should be getting first priority. How do we figure out which one?

Robin Lawton offers two customer roles and their corresponding definitions that greatly clear up this confusion:

- **End users.** These are people we had in mind when we designed the product. They will personally use the product to achieve a desired outcome. They are the most important customers.

- **Brokers.** These people do not personally use the product, but they transfer it to someone else who will use it. They act as an agent for either the end user or the producer. As an agent for the end user, the broker makes the product more accessible, easier to use, or more appealing. As an agent for the producer, the broker "encourages" the end user to accept the product.[1]

These definitions clarify things and allow us to solve our tax form problem. Tax forms were not designed so that we could have accountants. Tax preparers and Intuit are parasite industries that have emerged because we made the forms too hard for the end users.

---

[1] Robin L. Lawton, *Creating a Customer-Centered Culture: Leadership in Quality, Innovation, and Speed* (Milwaukee, Wis.: ASQC Quality Press, 1993), chap. 2, "Diffentiating Customers," www.imtC3.com.

In nearly every transaction, these two types of customers will be present. Our challenge is to ensure that the end users get first priority.

 Are Brokers Bad People?

Are brokers bad people? Absolutely not. We all act as brokers from time to time. For example, as a boss you may review the work of your staff before it goes on to the end users. It's actually possible to play the role of producer, broker, and end user all at the same time. I may produce a strategic plan, which I then give to my staff (I'm the broker here), and which I will also use myself (as the end user). It's only when brokers obscure our view of the end users or take priority over them that we have a problem.

A classic example of this is the state of radio today. It is virtually impossible to hear any music you like—or any music at all because of all the commercials. The end user of a song is the listener. However, the radio stations are more focused on the advertisers (brokers)—another classic case of following the money. Advertisers want a demographic of 14- to 34-year-olds, which is why all the stations play music geared for them. These choices have real consequences: end users, fleeing traditional radio, are opting for satellite radio (where there is a commercial-free station to meet the desires of every customer segment) or iPods in their cars. One need only look to what cable television did to network television to see how this game will end. End users will stand for being ignored for only so long before they find a way to win.

ICANT-CU

One of the best examples of how government gets this customer issue confused is attached to the back of your car. Who is the customer for a license plate? Before you answer that, look back at the definitions of end users and brokers.

Worksheet for License Plate Production

Widget: License plate

Producer:

End users:

Brokers:

The end users of a license plate are law enforcement—the people we originally had in mind when we designed the product. You, the driver, are a broker. You don't use the plate; instead, you drive it around for law enforcement to look at. If you think about it, a license plate is actually just a big receipt that you have bolted to your car to prove to law enforcement that you have paid your road taxes. DMV offices are also brokers; they pass the plate on to you, the driver.

I use this example because our failure to understand the two types of customers has real consequences. Many states have gone through license plate beautification initiatives during the past few years. My home state was no different. Deciding that the license plate was ugly and failed to adequately convey our image as a river playland, state notables formed the license plate beautification commission. This was no small affair: senators, representatives, the first lady, prominent artists, and the DMV director were all brought together to create a better design. Who do you suppose was not on the commission? Law enforcement—the end users. The figure on the next page shows the license plate.

The way license plates used to work was that the first letter on the plate was a code for the month of expiration and the big colored sticker in the middle represented the year of expiration. At seventy miles an hour, going the opposite direction, law enforcement could tell whether somebody had paid their road taxes (a fact I learned in focus groups with angry highway patrolmen). The beautification

New License Plate

commission decided the sticker was too ugly and detracted from the new artwork, so they relegated it to a tiny role in the bottom corner. The letter code for the month of expiration was too cumbersome for inventory practices, said the DMV, so they relegated the month to a tiny sticker on the other corner of the plate. A little artwork here, a few new colors there, and we have a beautiful plate. The only problem is that law enforcement has to be two feet away from the car at a dead stop to see if in fact the driver's road taxes are paid. Add the prevalence of personalized plates featuring photos of your dog wearing a sweatshirt from your alma mater, and you see why law enforcement can't even tell which state the car is from, much less if it's stolen or unregistered.

Here's where it gets real painful. In the focus groups with law enforcement, officers brought data demonstrating that the number of traffic stops for expired license plates dropped 50 percent with the introduction of the new, prettier plate. At a time when our highway system is crumbling and every possible dollar is needed, we reduced this enforcement mechanism by 50 percent.

How can so many people working together make so many mistakes in so short a time? A lack of understanding of this most vital concept of end users.

Perhaps no group struggles with this concept of customers more than regulators. They just seem to have a visceral reaction to the notion that the person they are doing something to is the person they should be doing something for. If we go back again to the environmental agency, we quickly see the conundrum. If we talk about customers in the abstract, independent of a specific widget, we get the following list of customers from the environmental regulators:

- environmentalists
- U.S Environmental Protection Agency (EPA)
- industry
- legislature
- Mother Earth
- neighbors
- staff
- taxpayers
- wildlife

With such a list, we obviously have competing interests. Who would you work to satisfy? (If the bear is big, I'm going with wildlife.) Now let's apply what we've learned and clear this up a bit. The environmental permit is the widget that, when used by customers, allows the agency to achieve results for its investors. Given that, we get the following:

- Widget: Environmental permit for a new manufacturing plant
- Producer: Permit staff
- End users: Plant manager, permit inspector, concerned neighbors
- Brokers: Permit consultants, attorneys, the legislature, EPA, others involved in writing the rules

So where does everybody else fit? They don't have a role in this widget.

One of the key things we have to learn to do is separate the customers of the widget (the permit) from those who care deeply about the outcome (clean air). Does that mean we ignore the environmentalists, Mother Earth, and the citizens as a whole? Only if we want to get fired. Remember, we exist to achieve results for our investors. We most certainly have to achieve those results. We have to ensure clean air. Right now, the way we do that is by creating a permit for our end users that helps them restrict pollutants.

The natural argument is that if we ask these customers what they want, they will tell us they don't want a permit at all. Too bad for them. They have to have a permit so that we can satisfy our investors. The same thing happens when Ford asks its customers what they want in a car. People say they want a free car. Too bad for them. Ford will do what it can to please the customer, but it can't give away cars and still please its investors.

The great challenge facing regulators is trying to satisfy two different sets of customers. Case in point: a nursing home license. The agency naturally says the customers of the license are the residents of the nursing home. Again, we have to ask which part of the license do they like best? Senior citizens and other residents are end users of the nursing home, not end users of the license. The end users of the license are the owner of the nursing home and the nursing home inspectors, both of which are trying to understand the terms and conditions of the license to ensure that the nursing home residents are getting good care. What role do residents play in the license? None. Does that mean the licensing agency should ignore residents of the nursing home? Absolutely not.

It is the great challenge of regulators to think globally and act locally. That is, not only do we have to create great widgets (permits, licenses, regulations), but also we have to ensure that the people we are regulating are also making great widgets (nursing homes, new houses, phone service). We have to keep our eyes on two sets of customers and ensure that the widgets we make for those we regulate truly help their customers. This is tough work. Again, that's why you are paid the big bucks. If it was easy, people from the private sector could do our jobs.

Follow the Money

This short exercise allows you to determine the customer roles and power relationships for any one of your key widgets.

While doing this exercise, you perhaps came across a startling discovery—the most important customers (the end users) had the least

Worksheet for Determining Customer Roles and Power Relationships for Specific Widgets

My widget:

My end users for that widget:

My brokers for that widget:

Who has the most power over the way the widget is currently designed?

Who has the least power over the way the widget is currently designed?

Why is this so?

power. This is not uncommon. Power is often determined by who controls the purse strings. One of the greatest sins we commit in government is licking the hands that feed us and biting the hands that we are supposed to be feeding. Food stamps are a great example of this, but the lesson can be applied to many widgets the government produces. The following shows the customer roles:

- Widget: Electronic benefit transfer (EBT) card

- Producer: Local food stamp office or third-party vendor

- End users: Low-income recipients, grocers

- Brokers: Congress, U.S. Department of Agriculture, state social services agency, contract monitors, auditors

How much power do the end users, particularly the low-income recipients, have over the widget? Zip. They are told what food they can buy, where they can buy it, how much they can spend, where they can get their card, and when they have to reapply. How happy do you think they are?

Who's calling the shots? Follow the money. Instead of worrying about providing great service to the end user, the local food stamp office focuses all its attention on ensuring the state agency and all its contract monitors and auditors are happy. Why? So the food stamp offices can keep their funding. The state agency, instead of worrying about whether local food stamp offices are providing great service to the end users, focuses all its attention on the U.S. Department of Agriculture's contract monitors and auditors. Why? So it can keep its funding. And the USDA, of course, rather than worrying about whether states are providing great service to the end users, focuses all of its attention on Congress and Congress's monitors and auditors. Why? So USDA can keep its funding. Everybody is looking upward toward the funding sources. No wonder the end users feel like they are being looked down upon.

Great managers find a way to keep everybody happy—the end users, the brokers, and the investors. The first step is getting clear about who's who. Now we have to figure out what they want.

Customer Surveys Are Suitable for Wrapping Fish

One of the most common excuses I get from agency managers for why they don't need to improve is that their survey scores are good. "If our surveys show that 90 percent of customers are satisfied, aren't we doing all right?" You are, for meatloaf.

Have you ever been to a friend's house for dinner and they served you meatloaf? (You have to question the friendship at this point.) At the end of the meal, your gracious host turns to you and says, "How was it?" Of course you reply, "It was good," finishing the sentence—"for meatloaf"—only to yourself. It was good, for meatloaf. I don't expect much out of meatloaf, and you nailed it. The same is often true of our survey scores.

Our customers (provided we even get to the right ones) return them with high marks—their way of saying, "You make a fine meatloaf." They didn't expect much from government, and we exceeded those expectations. We can exceed customers' expectations and not

BOX 4.6 **One Size Does Not Fit All**

When you are comfortable with the concept of end users and brokers, you will also quickly see that they are not homogeneous groups. That is, not all end users are the same. In our Ford example, the end users of a car break out into many segments defined by gender, income, age, size of family, and planned use for the car. It is virtually impossible to build one car that can satisfy all of these segments. That's why Ford builds all the different models it does.

Our government end users are also not one-size-fits-all. But, unfortunately, we tend to treat them that way, which results in two things—dissatisfaction on their part and waste on ours. To access most social services, for example, all end users follow the same route. They have to find transportation to get to an office where they have to stand in line and wait to speak to someone or be interviewed. This is a very expensive (for government and for the customer) service delivery model. For some end users, it is the appropriate model. But what about seniors and the disabled? What about the single mom who works all day? What about those who are Internet savvy?

Rather than offering only one-size-fits-all, governments could offer choices. Services could be accessed in a self-service model, a moderate-support model, and an intensive-care model. Forcing intensive-care customers into a self-service model is cruel. Forcing self-service people into an intensive-care model is also cruel.

be anywhere close to giving them what they want because customers' expectations are based on their experiences.

We have become conditioned to expect our flights to be late, our DMV lines to be long, and the checkout registers at Wal-Mart to be understaffed. It's what we expect, but is it really what we want? Our good survey scores lull us into a false sense of accomplishment.

Surveys are absolutely everywhere and not just in government. I recently stayed in a hotel room that asked me to fill out three separate surveys: one in the bedroom, one in the TV room, and one in the bathroom (you've got to hand it to them on that one—they had a captive audience). It seems that every organization that embraces the get-close-to-the-customer mantra immediately does a customer survey. So what's wrong with that?

Let me ask you this: Do you survey your spouse? Probably not. All the management gurus will tell you that the key to building a long-term meaningful relationship with your customers is to do a survey. Yet in that other area of your life where you are trying to create such a relationship, you don't survey. Why not? Because you intuitively know that there is a better way.

My personal opinion is that customer surveys are generally suitable for wrapping fish. (For more on this topic, see my article "Are Your Surveys Generally Suitable for Wrapping Fish?" in the December 1998 edition of *Quality Progress*.)

Typical surveys

- ask the wrong questions of
- the wrong people
- at the wrong time
- for the wrong reasons.

The Wrong Questions

Following is a typical survey one might find in a hotel room:

Is it possible that you could mark "satisfied" for all the questions listed and still not be satisfied? What is the number one outcome a business traveler would like from a hotel stay? It is probably a good night's sleep. (This is why it is important to segment your customers. A good night's sleep is unlikely to be a high priority for honeymooners.) You can have a clean room with friendly service, a nice remote control, and fluffy pillows, but if all night long the elevator keeps dinging and the ice from the ice machine keeps falling (you do realize that the government-rate rooms are all across from the vending machines and the elevators, right?), you will not be satisfied.

Example of Hotel Satisfaction Survey

Satisfaction Survey

	Excellent		Good		Poor
How would you rate our staff?					
Front desk	5	4	3	2	1
Housekeeping	5	4	3	2	1
Room service	5	4	3	2	1
Restaurant services	5	4	3	2	1
How would you rate our:					
Front desk services	5	4	3	2	1
Check-in efficiency	5	4	3	2	1
Check-out efficiency	5	4	3	2	1
How would you rate:					
Bathroom cleanliness	5	4	3	2	1
Bedroom cleanliness	5	4	3	2	1
Television	5	4	3	2	1
Heat/air conditioning	5	4	3	2	1
Lighting	5	4	3	2	1
Overall, how would you rate your stay?	5	4	3	2	1

What could we do to make your stay more pleasant next time?

Although "good night's sleep" is the number one priority of business travelers, no one ever asks about it on hotel surveys. Why not? This is no great mystery if you think about how most surveys are created. A team gets locked in a room and can't get out until a survey is created. Usually there isn't a customer in sight. At best, with these surveys, all we are discovering is how satisfied customers are with things we think they think are important.

The right way to find out what customers want is to ask them, but not in a survey. Organizations can learn more from their customers in a ninety-minute focus group or a fifteen-minute interview than they will ever find out in a decade of surveys. Surveys can be adequate tools to measure how well we are doing on the things customers care about. But they are a horrible way to figure out the things customers care about in the first place.

Quite often organizations confuse lack of dissatisfaction with satisfaction. A hotel survey may ask whether I was satisfied with the plumbing. After enough good marks for plumbing, they may throw themselves a pizza party. But is the quality of the plumbing a satisfier for me? That is, when I flush the toilet in a hotel bathroom and the water goes down the hole, do I jump up and down for joy and declare my undying loyalty to that hotel? No. I expect it. When you expect something and get it, it's no big deal. It's not a satisfier. When I expect something and don't get it—if the water in the toilet comes back toward me when I flush—then I'm dissatisfied. We can remove all the things that dissatisfy our customers, and all we've done is make them less angry. (Sometimes in government this is a lofty enough goal.) The absence of dissatisfaction does not equal satisfaction.

Frederick Herzberg made this exact point about employee satisfaction.[2] Take a minute to jot down the five things that bug you most about your current job—the things that really aggravate you. (I am guessing you put down things like computer problems, no parking, unrealistic deadlines, office politics, pay, and so on.) Now, suppose all of those items were eliminated; they somehow have been solved. Would you be satisfied? Would you skip into work saying, "Thank God It's Monday"? Not likely. What would make you do cartwheels coming into your office? I am sure your list would look quite different—feeling like you made a difference, having a challenging assignment, working with a great team, and other similar things.

Like customer surveys, most employee surveys also focus on dissatisfiers, and they fail to see that all we are doing is making people less angry, not more happy. With customers, as well as employees, it is not enough to remove the items that cause dissatisfaction; we must also replace them with items that lead to satisfaction.

The Wrong People

With the hotel room survey, it's not too hard to ensure you are surveying the right people. But in many other cases the situation can be

---

[2] Frederick Herzberg, "One More Time: How Do You Motivate Employees?" *Harvard Business Review* 46 (January-February 1968).

far more difficult. If you are Xerox and you sell copiers, whom do you survey? The person who buys the copier, the person who installs the copier, the person who uses the copier, or the person who kicks the copier every time it jams? If you say we should survey all of them, then who should get top priority if they have competing interests?

If you are a health insurance provider, whom do you survey? The employer that buys the policy, the employee, the employee's family, the doctor, the hospital? If all of them, who gets priority? If you are a bank regulator, whom do you survey? The bank, the legislature, the citizens who use the banks? Who should get priority? This takes us right back to where we started with this chapter. If we don't know who the customer is and what role the customer is playing (end user vs. broker), a survey certainly isn't going to help us out.

The Wrong Time

One of the big problems with surveys is that they are reactive. Although the guest turns in the hotel survey, that person is already gone and there is little the hotel can do to increase that guest's satisfaction. TQM became popular in manufacturing because it challenged the common practice of trying to inspect quality in a product. Traditional manufacturing practices had a quality assurance department that caught defects before they went out the door, but by the time defects made it to quality assurance many resources had been wasted. At the heart of TQM was the idea that we need to build in quality upfront—by knowing what customers want, designing the widget accordingly, and building fail-safe processes that minimize the potential for defects.

Although most organizations have learned this lesson on the shop floor, they are still applying the old logic to surveys. Quality cannot be surveyed into a widget. Organizations must instead take the steps to build quality into their widgets from the very beginning. The right time to survey is after determining what customers want. Then you design the widget to meet those expectations.

The Wrong Reason

Any customer inquiry method should be for the purpose of driving action, that is, to learn specifically what customers want so that you can make it happen. Unfortunately most surveys are not used for learning; instead, they are used for keeping score.

A major shift has occurred at car dealerships. Car companies decided they wanted their sales staffs to be nice to customers, not just sell cars. To show how serious they were, they shifted the sales staff's compensation to also take into account customer survey scores. During one recent car-buying experience, while I was waiting in the office as my salesperson pretended to run my counteroffer by the sales manager, I noticed an enlarged copy of their dealer satisfaction survey posted in blow-up size on the wall. All the categories were filled in with "highly satisfied." I guess it was supposed to subliminally trick me into thinking I was highly satisfied. To top it off, when the transaction was complete and I was ready to walk out the door, my salesperson gave me a copy of the survey—already filled out!—and remarked that I was undoubtedly a busy man and wouldn't have time to fill it out myself. The assumption of course was that I was "highly satisfied" in all categories, but I was told I could request another one to take with me to fill out later, blah, blah, blah. What was the purpose of all that? To truly understand what makes me tick? To hold the dealers accountable? I make it a habit to never, ever fill out surveys. Perhaps you should, too.

So, surveys ask the wrong questions, of the wrong people, at the wrong time, and they don't drive action. Other than that, they are perfect.

So what can we do if we can't survey our customers? Hold on to your seats, I'm going to offer a radical idea here: Go talk to them! Spend time with them! (I'll now give you a moment to pull yourself together.) We want to be proactive and know what customers want (not what they've been conditioned to expect) so we can build successful widgets.

My first week on the job at the DMV, I went incognito and just watched the flow of customer traffic. It was fascinating to see how customers came in, where they went, and what they looked at. One of the biggest problems that DMVs encounter is that people continually get in the wrong lines. It's bad enough to wait 45 minutes in line, but to do it twice is enough to incite violence. At that time, the DMV offices were considering a new sign initiative to correct the problem. They were going to invest close to $1 million across the state to put up large—the size of McDonald's menu board—signs directing people to one side to get a driver's license and to the other side to register their cars. What I noticed by watching customers, however, was that they never ever looked up. Something about a DMV office makes people want to avoid eye contact at all costs. When I shared this observation with the manager, she said she had noticed it, too, and had thought about putting signs on the floor.

The next day we tried it. Using a few pieces of paper and magic marker, we taped directional signs on the floor. For a grand total of about 20 cents, customers started getting in the right lines. It's amazing what you can learn if you just spend time with your customers. Get out of your office and go see them—now. I'll be here when you get back.

Welcome back. The tax form team I mentioned earlier in the chapter was having a difficult time convincing staff that the forms needed to be improved. The general response was, "If those dummies would just read the instructions, they wouldn't have so much trouble." So the team decided to assemble a bunch of the dummies in a room and have them do their taxes in front of the smarties. After 20 minutes, the exercise had to be stopped for the safety of everyone involved. Most participants didn't get past line 2. Needless to say, attitudes changed quickly.

In my other book, *The Change Agent's Guide to Radical Improvement*, I share the step-by-step focus group process and questions we use to always find out what customers want even if they don't know it themselves. It's too much detail to get into here, but it is simple enough that hundreds of government managers have been able to do it themselves.

 BOX 4.7   Do You Want Fries with That?

A common argument I get when I talk to managers about customer satisfaction is: "We already have a customer service program." That's great—you've tackled 4 percent of the issue.

continued

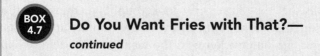

Do You Want Fries with That?—
continued

Customer service is not the same as customer satisfaction. Suppose it was your time to head to the DMV. If you are like most people, you will take an hour of vacation time and go at the end of the work day. After your fifteen-minute drive and your forty-five-minute wait in line, you will inevitably learn at the counter that you have failed to bring sundry information such as your grandmother's birth certificate, your proof of rubella vaccination, and your proof that your pet has been spayed or neutered. You then scamper out of the DMV office to gather these things in hopes of making it back before closing time. The next morning, you again take an hour of vacation to be the first in line when they open.

The principles of customer service emphasize that when you get to the counter that next morning, the DMV employee will smile a big smile and say with all possible sincerity, "Hi, welcome to the DMV. How may I be of service to you today?" What's wrong with that? Nothing. It's great, but it's only a slim slice of the whole customer satisfaction pie.

Customer service seeks to improve how humans (the staff) interact with other humans (the customers). Customer satisfaction takes a much broader view. It asks different questions:

- Why do customers have to wait so long in line?

- Why do customers have to bring in all this information?

- Why do customers have to come in at all?

- Why can't customers do this from home?

To this day I still get comments from people about how friendly the DMV staff are in the offices we improved. Guess how much we spent on customer service training? Zero. It's amazing how friendly the staff can be when the customers aren't yelling at them.

When you spend time with customers uncovering what they want, some clear patterns emerge. Whether you are talking about a car, a cell phone, an appendectomy, a building permit, a foster care placement, a Medicaid plan, a water hookup, or a police report, customers tend to care about five things: ease of use, timeliness, accuracy, cost, and choice.[3]

Ease of use. Perhaps no company understands ease of use better than Apple. Apple has created a growing fan base of loyal users because Apple products are so simple to use. (I should disclose that I am an Apple stockholder, so please buy more Apple products.) What can we in government learn from companies like Apple? Plenty.

One of the reasons the iPod took over the world was that it so easily integrated the hardware and the software. Now, in one place, I could store all my songs, buy new songs, research new bands, and check out recommendations of people who liked the same bands I liked. It was not just one-stop shopping, it was shopping that anticipated my needs and helped me find what would be helpful to me.

One of the most frequent projects I work on is service integration in government. That is, how do we take a fragmented set of services, trapped in five different organizational silos, and make it easy for the customer. In one locality, working with an awesome staff, we built a virtual "working-poor store." The team lived with the analogy of a specialty store just for the working poor, where they could walk in and everything they would need was already there for them, prepackaged and ready to go. No need to hunt and search—just get what you need, get everything you need, and have it customized for you. We worked intently with the working poor. We uncovered their wants and the widgets they needed to meet those wants and then built the systems necessary to ensure they got everything they needed in one visit, and we made sure they knew who to contact if they ever needed anything else.

One of the most amazing inventions of our time are the portable heart defibrillators that now hang close to fire extinguishers in many public spaces. The gentleman who designed these had a simple goal:

---

[3] Robin L. Lawton, *Creating a Customer-Centered Culture: Leadership in Quality, Innovation, and Speed* (Milwaukee, Wis: ASQC Quality Press, 1993), chap. 3, "Defining Customer Expectations," www.imtC3.com.

make it so easy to use that a six-year-old could save someone's life. He made an idiot-proof life-saving device, but I'll bet he still can't do his own taxes.

Timeliness. It's pretty easy to figure out when customers want things: yesterday. When do I want my computer fixed? Right now. When do I want my expense account check? Yesterday. When do I want my performance appraisal? Never. Oops. For customers the clock starts when they want something and ends when they get it (done correctly). Often in government we start the clock when we get something from citizens done correctly (like a food stamp application), and we end the clock whenever the statute tells us we have to.

BOX 4.8 **Reset Your Clocks**

Human resources (HR) functions often have well-developed performance measures. One of the most frequent measures they will use is "time to hire." Unfortunately, the clock starts on their measures when they post the position and ends when the job is filled. Customers—the hiring managers—have a far different expectation. Their measure of timeliness is the number of days that the job is not filled. The clock starts for them the second they know someone is planning to leave. How would this measure change the practices of HR?

But Dell, FedEx, and TiVo have combined to totally warp our view of time. As customers, we are now conditioned to be able to get what we want whenever we want it. That is part of the reason people get so frustrated with government. They know what is possible. There are few things government does that couldn't benefit from being done faster (80 percent faster, at least).

Accuracy. Gone are the days when people's purchase decisions were primarily based on quality. Perfection used to be a differentiator in the marketplace. Now it is a given. We assume what we buy will work, period. Six Sigma set a high standard in manufacturing for perfection: four parts per million could be defective. This level of technical quality is astounding and is being achieved in plant after plant. Unfortunately this same level of accuracy has not been demanded of the 85 percent of the employees in these companies who don't make widgets. How much better would life be if only four answers out a million were allowed to be incorrect? Or four bills or invoices out of a million?

Cost. Cost is not to be confused with price. What we pay for a widget may reflect only a portion of the total cost. How much did your car cost? For the real costs, add to the sticker price the cost of interest, insurance, gasoline, oil changes, tires, and those little pine trees you hang on the rearview mirror. Now add the time you spent researching cars, travel time, negotiation time, and a settlement for pain and suffering, and you come up with the real bottom line.

In government, we are often leery of price hikes because they look like tax increases, but you would be amazed at what customers will pay in price to avoid paying large costs. The price of a driver's license, for example, is around $15.00. The total cost, including drive time, waiting in line, taking an hour off of work, and so forth, could run into the hundreds. A reform we implemented with the DMV was to double the price of the license while cutting the costs in half. We stretched the life of the license from three years to six years, but we halved the costs to customers even though the prices of the licenses went up. We never heard a peep of dissatisfaction.

Regulatory agencies are often at odds with their industries over permit fees. But in the focus groups I conducted with businesses, they said they were more than willing to pay up to five times as much in permit fees if the agency would just go faster. Why? Because their costs for downtime far exceeded the nominal price of the permit. Many progressive regulatory agencies we have worked with will implement the FedEx model of pricing: if you want it overnight, it'll cost more. Customers have the choice.

Choice. Choice is one of the customer's greatest wants. I once was working with some Eastern Europeans right after the fall of the Berlin Wall. At one point we stopped in a small store to pick up some

Myth 2: We Don't Have Customers

Why it matters:

- Just as the widget is the link between our factory and our customers, the customer is the link between our widget and our outcomes. That is, the only way we achieve our outcomes is if the customer can successfully use our widget. All factories have widgets, all widgets have customers.

- Confusion about who the customer is leads to misplaced priorities. We have multiple customers with competing interests. Those with power and purse strings tend to dictate how the widget will be. Often the real users are left out and are stuck with ineffective, unsatisfying widgets such as license plates that cannot be read at a distance by law enforcement officers.

- We are public servants, and we exist to serve. Helping employees connect with and satisfy their end users makes for a culture of service.

- Dissatisfied customers yell a lot (at employees, at elected officials, and to the media).

The truth:

We do have customers—specifically end users of the widgets we produce. It is our obligation to ensure that we understand the priorities of our multiple customers who have competing interests and that we work to satisfy the end users first.

---

toothpaste. There were two choices: a brown box and an orange box. I asked the shopkeeper which one sold better. He said that the orange outsold the brown ten to one, even though it cost a tiny bit more. Why? For decades there had been only a brown box.

My company did extensive work with a mental health system to uncover issues customers were having with the care provided to the

What to measure:

How well the customers were able to achieve their desired outcomes

How well we are meeting customer priorities:

- ease of use (number of minutes to complete a form)
- timeliness (number of days to receive a permit)
- accuracy (percentage of payments correct the first time)
- cost (number of days of lost productivity)
- choice (percentage of customers using Internet transactions)

How to improve:

- Talk with customers to determine their expectations for the widget; be proactive.
- Develop objective measures for customer priorities.
- Work with customers to assign numerical targets for the measures (e.g., receive a permit in two days).
- Identify ways to close the gap between the customer-desired target and current government performance; use innovation to develop alternative widgets that could better achieve customer outcomes.
- Involve employees in the improvement process.

mentally retarded and developmentally disabled. The perception was that the level of care was inadequate and what was needed was massive outsourcing to privatized vendors. Focus groups with parents and families, and with the patients when feasible, revealed a totally different problem. They were satisfied with the quality of care they received by state employees, but they were dissatisfied at the level of control they had over receiving that care. The families wanted some choices and some say over what their children were receiving, how often, and where. Their desire for choice produced changes in the system dramatically different from simply privatizing.

But the most important thing customers want is results. We don't buy products; we buy results. We don't buy cars; we buy transportation. We don't buy drills; we buy holes. We don't buy cologne; we buy hope. Our challenge is to ensure not only that our widgets are timely, easy to use, accurate, inexpensive, and customized but also that they achieve the results for which they were created. That is the subject of the next chapter.

Chapter

We're Not Here to Make a Profit

How would you manage differently if you were as focused on results as the private sector is focused on profit?

Imagine sitting in front of a budget committee and making the following statement: "We are not here to achieve results." Ouch. However, that is the exact statement we are making when we say government is not here to make a profit. Profit is simply the private sector's way of measuring outcomes. That is why there are no boring classes in the private sector on outcome measurement. They have just one—profit.

This is more than a semantic trick. It gets at the heart of the way we so often think in government. What we are really saying when we say we're not here to make a profit is that there is no built-in incentive to improve. A profit-making enterprise has to innovate or die because it is driven by the natural force of competition and the necessity of providing a high return to its investors. Are we really that different?

Parallels between Government and Private Business

	Business	Government
↑	Investors	Taxpayers
Accountability	Board of directors	Government board or legislature
	CEO	County manager or state governor
	Business unit	Department or division
	Products or services	Products or services

You'll recall the above graphic from the previous chapter. Like a business, government has investors—the taxpayers. Those taxpayers would like to earn higher returns on their investments. Those returns are not measured in dollars but in other ways—for example, new jobs created, an increase in affordable housing, and reduced instances of crime. It is our responsibility to deliver higher returns year after year, just like the private sector.

Imagine if we were as focused on those results as the private sector is on profit. We could communicate our value to investors, focus our attention on the right things to improve, and develop innovative alternatives that bring in even more results.

Communicating Our Value

Communicating with investors is not that hard. When I worked for an economic development agency, I had the pleasure of meeting a very wealthy venture capitalist. This man heard pitch after pitch from people looking for money. Our group asked him what he listened for in these presentations. His answer was so simple: "If I give you one dollar, how many dollars do I get back?"

In my life, I have had the great ... pleasure ... to sit through numerous budget hearings. I'm always amazed at what they concentrate on. Are there great discussions about the impact the agency is having on the world? Are there careful analyses of return on investment so that the elected officials can make informed investment decisions? Are there discussions of bold strategic alternatives in anticipation of a shifting marketplace? No. It's usually about how many miles a fleet car should have on it before it gets replaced. Why is that? Who is to blame?

"All right," you say, "I'll grant you the analogy that taxpayers are like shareholders or investors. But the analogy breaks down because shareholders all agree and want the same thing—profit. Our government shareholders all want different things. Some want more investment in roads; others want investments in schools. Some want us to stop investing period."

But you are only assuming that all corporate shareholders want the same thing. That is simply not true. Some want high dividends and a steady stream of income. Others want earnings plowed back into the company to accelerate growth. Some want the company to stick to its knitting and keep delivering steady results. Others pressure the company to be bold and take risks. And, based on these desires, they elect a board of directors that best reflects the will of the majority of shareholders. Are we really so different?

The blame falls on both the legislators and the agencies, and it may be a chicken-and-egg scenario. Elected officials stop asking the big questions because they can't get satisfactory answers. Agency heads stop talking about the big questions because they keep getting asked the small ones. In any case, the culprit is the same—you can't control what you can't measure. Because elected officials can't see our results, they focus on what they can see—our expenditures.

This phenomenon is not restricted to agency heads and elected officials. Middle managers have the same troubles as they petition their bosses for additional resources. If we are ever to shift the conversation to the more important things, we've got to find a way to communicate our value. From this I've created Ken Miller's "law of budgeting": The less our value is understood, the more our funding is scrutinized.

So, why can't we communicate our value? Part of the problem is not understanding the system of work. Without this framework in place, we struggle to know what to measure and communicate. Investors want to know outcomes. Instead, we often give them what they don't want to know.

System of Work

Factory   Widget   Customers   Outcomes

- **Activities.** How many inspection visits we performed, how many calls we answered, and how many full-time employees worked how many hours, for example. Imagine the CEO of Ford presenting the quarterly earnings statement by saying, "We had 8,000 employees working to take orders, handle raw materials, and build cars."

- **Volume of widgets produced.** How many audits were completed, how many permits were issued, how many potholes were filled, for example. Again, imagine the CEO of Ford telling Ford's investors, "With your money this year, we built 500,000 cars."

- **Number of customers served.** How many food stamp clients were served, how many participants came in for training, how many probation cases were supervised, for example. Imagine the CEO of Ford telling company investors that Ford had served more than 300,000 people during the year.

What's wrong with sharing these things? Nothing, except investors don't care. The CEO of Ford can share how many people he employed, how many cars Ford built, and how many customers Ford served, but all the investors care about is how much money Ford made doing all of that. That is the most important question. Is it because, as Gordon Gecko said, "Greed is good"? No, it is because it's the role of the board of directors to ensure that the current business is the best use of the investors' money. Investors may love Ford cars, and Ford people, and the legacy of Ford to America, but if making cars doesn't make money, investors have a moral obligation to shift those investments to other endeavors. To do otherwise only harms all investors and wastes capital that could be used to grow our economy. (For more on this topic please watch the cinematic "masterpiece" *Other People's Money,* starring Danny DeVito.) Government's comparable board of directors has that same obligation—to shift resources where they do the most good.

Measuring Outcomes

Saying we have to demonstrate our value is easy. Doing it in government is incredibly difficult. Understanding that we are here to achieve a profit (results), and understanding the system of work can be an enormous help in this endeavor. Another tool I have found helpful is the age-old process of asking five whys.

This tool gets us out of the box. It forces us to think not about what we do, but why we do it. For example, a job-training agency may have a widget called a job-training program. Sure, we can track how many people attended the program, how much we spent, and

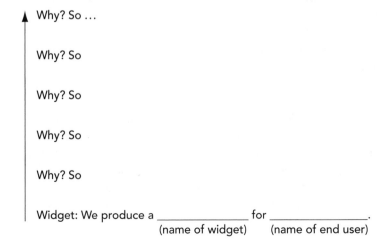

The Five Whys

Why? So …

Why? So

Why? So

Why? So

Why? So

Widget: We produce a _____ for _____.
                     (name of widget)   (name of end user)

how happy the participants were, but what the investors care about are the results we got from the program.

Although most people use five-whys thinking to drill down and solve a problem, we use it to look up and find our true purpose:

- Why? So they can support their family.

- Why? So they can obtain a higher wage.

- Why? So they can keep the job.

- Why? So they can get a job.

- Why? So they can increase their skills.

- We produce a job-training program for job seekers.

What you see is that (1) this way of thinking quickly gets us off what we do and focuses on why we do it, and (2) there are multiple levels of results. It is our job next to figure out which levels in the hierarchy we want to be responsible for and then attach measures to those. In this case, program staff may decide that they will be responsible for getting people jobs at a higher wage but that tracking whether they can support their families is out of their control and would not provide useful management information.

After they decide which outcome level to focus on, the staff can then track which new skills the attendees acquire; how many get jobs; how many keep those jobs for six months, twelve months, and into the future; and the attendees' wages before they entered the program and after.

The table on the next page shows some outcome measures for common government widgets.

Now that I've said all of this, let me state: I'm just not a big fan of the outcome measurement movement. I'm reminded of Jeff Goldblum's character in the movie *Jurassic Park,* who remarked upon learning about the creation of the new dinosaurs, "You were so busy trying to figure out if you could do something that you never stopped to ask whether you should." Just because you can find a way to measure an outcome doesn't always mean you should. The value of a measure is determined by its usage. The only good measures are the ones we use. Unfortunately, most outcome measurement exercises

Examples of Outcome Measures for Common Government Widgets

Widget	Outcome measure
Company relocation proposal	Percentage won, number of new jobs created or retained
Export matches	Number of net new dollars of export sales
Medicaid plan	Percentage of citizens with health coverage
Food stamps and temporary assistance for needy families (TANF)	Percentage of families moving up self-sufficiency index
Child abuse investigation reports	Percentage of repeat offenders
Building permits	Number of affordable housing units available
Code inspection reports	Number of repeat violators
Mental health treatment plans	Percentage of patients meeting treatment goals
Inmate GED program	Percentage of inmates employed upon release
Probation visits	Recidivism rate
Computer repairs	Number of hours of lost work time

are just that—exercises that produce measures that we can place in forms that nobody looks at. They don't help us manage the business.

Many states spend a lot of money on measuring health indicators like the infant mortality rates or incidences of diseases. For epidemiologists, this can be fun work. For managers and elected officials, these indicators offer little to no value. How many years do you think have to pass before there is any movement in the infant mortality rate of a state or locality? It's like watching paint dry. Some governments even try to make each program attempt to prove its impact on the infant mortality rate. Absurd. Most outcome measures are rarely used because they don't tell us anything anytime soon.

BOX 5.2 **Value of Enforcement**

Measuring outcomes in enforcement-related activities is a tricky business, but it can also have amazing effects. Quite often, government enforcers (like building inspectors, permit inspectors, auditors, and compliance monitors) will measure success by the number of enforcements given (for example, the number of violations found or the number of audit findings). Is that truly the purpose of government enforcement? Do we want more violations? More audit findings?

What is the purpose of an audit? To find areas of noncompliance. Why? So that compliance replaces noncompliance. If our true purpose is to help people comply, then our goal should be zero enforcement actions. What would you do differently if that was your goal?

One time a colleague shared this goal with a group of tax auditors. They had been measuring their success on the basis of the number of audits completed and dollars collected. They were trying to find things that were wrong. When this goal was replaced with "percentage of repeat findings per industry"—a simple measurement change—it forced a total change in thinking and strategy. The auditors had to find the common issues in each industry and then proactively educate the companies so that they would not continue to make these mistakes. If the auditors were successful, what they found in one company should not be found anywhere else.

The tax auditors really hated this idea.

There are also areas where it is simply futile to try to measure outcomes. Administrative functions, in particular. We absolutely want the procurement unit to measure how long they take, how many orders they get right the first time, and how satisfied customers are. But do we really want them to try to prove their impact on the citizenry?

My favorite exercises in futility are the attempts to get prevention organizations to measure what didn't happen: crimes that didn't occur, fires that didn't burn, banks that didn't fail. Further, the efforts of many prevention programs, like public service announcements or community education efforts, are lost among the millions of different variables that can affect the outcome. Are we really going to credit the stop-smoking brochure for the decline in teen smoking?

If an outcome measure is useful to you—that is, if it helps you communicate, inspire, or learn—then go for it. If not, please don't. What we need in government is less outcome measurement and more outcome thinking, less strategic planning and more strategic thinking. (doing)

BOX 5.3   **Five Important Questions**

Every leader should be asking the following five questions:

1. What results are we trying to achieve?

2. How would we know if we were achieving them?

3. What strategies are we using to achieve the results?

4. Are these strategies working?

5. What do we need to do differently to achieve our results?

Focusing Our Attention on the Right Things

When we don't use outcome thinking, we tend to focus our attention on the other parts of the system-of-work model. Typically we get highly wrapped up inside the factory, worrying about how we do things and forgetting about why we do them in the first place. Peter Drucker said, "There is nothing so useless as doing efficiently that which should not be done at all."[1] It is to this topic that we now turn.

Innovative government. This is not an oxymoron. It is a mandate. As I have stated repeatedly throughout this book: The way we

---

[1] Peter F. Drucker, *The Essential Drucker: The Best of Sixty Years of Peter Drucker's Essential Writings on Management* (New York: Collins, 2003).

achieve results is by building better widgets for customers in more efficient factories. If we want different results, we have to build different widgets. It's that simple. Widgets are how our mission statements, strategic plans, initiatives, collaborative partnerships, and everything else that is just talk become tangible.

At some point it is our job as leaders to ask, "Is this widget the best way to achieve these outcomes?"

- Are nursing home licenses the best way to ensure quality care in nursing homes?

- Are educational standards the best way to improve school performance?

 BOX 5.4   **Competitive Libraries**

When you think of libraries, you probably picture rows upon rows of old books and someone telling you to be quiet. Actually, libraries are on the cutting edge of innovation in government. They have to be. The profit measure for libraries is circulation—how much stuff gets checked out. With the rise of companies like Google and Amazon and the technology to be able to read virtually any book anytime from anywhere, libraries are fast becoming obsolete. This challenge is causing radical rethinking of the very purpose of the library. Are we here to check out books and magazines or to help people access knowledge? If the answer is accessing knowledge, what should we be doing differently? If our true purpose is to increase literacy in the community, what should we be doing differently?

One progressive manager of a large county library system I worked with has instituted customer councils that are organized by customer segment—teens, seniors, moms with small children, for example—to help govern the libraries and customize offerings to those segments so that they truly are increasing knowledge and literacy in the communities they serve.

- Are performance-based budgets the best way to improve government agencies?

- Are food subsidies the best way to help families support themselves?

- Are tax forms the best way to collect taxes?

If we were as profit driven as the private sector, we would ask this question about our government widgets all the time. Except the private sector doesn't always ask these questions either. Here are three of my favorite blunders.

- **TDK.** I was on an airplane in the mid-1990s reading the in-flight magazine when I stumbled upon an interview with the CEO of TDK. I can't remember his name, and I'm sure plenty of people would like to forget it. In this interview, the writer asked, "We are entering the digital area. Compact discs, DVDs, even digital music seem to be on the horizon. As the leader in the audiotape industry, what are you doing as a company to prepare for these changes?" I couldn't believe the response. "We at TDK are the leaders in audiotapes. We produce consistent, high-quality products that our customers have come to trust. People will always have a need for audiotapes. We're going to stick to our core business." I've never come so close to using the AirFone. The $20 call would have been worth it to warn the passengers on the SS *TDK* that their captain had seen the iceberg and was heading straight for it at top speed. TDK was not the leader in CDs, nor did it invent the iPod.

- **Stuckey's.** Any of you who have traveled the highways that cut across Middle America have probably seen Stuckey's, or at least their decaying exoskeletons. Many of you may have stopped in for a pecan log a time or two. Littered across the highway system are these monuments to strategic error. When the highway system was first constructed, Stuckey's was the place you stopped to go to the bathroom, grab a snack, or get a snow globe featuring the local landmark. The only thing you couldn't get there was ... gas. Faced with the decision whether to add gas pumps to their stores, they decided that wasn't the business they were in.

- **Franklin.** Many of you may be reformed Franklin planner users. Franklin had a neat little cult of people who spent as much time organizing their lives as living them. With their goal pages, and inserts, and tabs, and rulers, and accessories galore, becoming organized had never been so much fun. And it wasn't just Franklin; there were Day-Runner, Day-Timer, and many others filling entire shelves at office supply stores. At those same office supply stores today, you can find all of these things in the 99 cent barrel. Franklin didn't invent the PalmPilot (although Franklin invented a way to print out your PalmPilot calendar and stick it in your Franklin, which entirely defeated the purpose of the PalmPilot), nor did Franklin invent the BlackBerry. In fact, Palm didn't invent the BlackBerry either. By the time you read this, BlackBerry might be out of business because it missed the next innovation.

What happens? How do such great companies go blind so quickly? Simply, they get so consumed building better widgets for their customers in more efficient factories that they forget their purpose. The purpose of TDK audiotapes was to help listeners enjoy music on the go. The purpose of Stuckey's was to refresh travelers and help them on their way. The purpose of Franklin planners was to help everyone stay organized and be productive. Here are some other dying widgets. See if you can figure out their purpose and their replacement.

- American Automobile Association (AAA)
- billboards
- copiers
- film
- glasses
- greeting cards
- keys
- lawn mowers
- overhead projectors
- pharmaceuticals
- stamps
- tax forms
- *TV Guide*
- video rentals
- yellow pages

We can't afford to make the same mistakes in government. True, we won't go out of business. We will just hang around being ineffective.

How do we get innovative? It actually has nothing to do with creativity. When we think of innovation, we envision artsy people in glass buildings or scientists in lab coats. That's not what innovation is about. Innovation is a way of thinking. Robin Lawton offers the most helpful definition: "Innovation is the process of making a desired outcome easier to obtain."[2] We stay innovative by focusing on outcomes.

The same five-whys thinking we used to develop outcome measures is also what we use to help us develop innovations. Starting with our widget, we work our way up the chain of whys until we reach motherhood and apple pie. The following example is for a performance appraisal.

Innovative Performance Appraisals

Why? So everybody is happy, there is a chicken in every pot, and we're all singing kumbaya.

Why? So we can achieve the goals of our organization.

Why? So we can achieve the goals of our unit.

Why? So employees can make improvements.

Why? So employees will know how well they are doing.

Why? So employees can get feedback on their performance.

Widget: We produce a performance appraisal for employees.

---

[2] Robin L. Lawton, *Creating a Customer-Centered Culture: Leadership in Quality, Innovation, and Speed* (Milwaukee, Wis.: ASQC Quality Press, 1993), chap. 5, "Quality and Innovation," www.imtC3.com.

We often hear the phrase, "Get out of the box." Well, what is the box? The diagram on the previous page shows it. The box is the smallest purpose. We produce performance appraisals to give employees feedback. Innovative, out-of-the-box thinking works as follows:

1. Is a performance appraisal the best way to give employees feedback?
2. Is there anything else we can do to give employees feedback?

At this point we're still in the box.

3. Is our true purpose to give employees feedback or to help them improve?
4. If we were in the helping-employees-improve business, which widgets would we create?

Now we're out of the box.

5. Is our true purpose to help employees improve or help the unit achieve its goals?
6. If we're in the help-the-unit-achieve-its-goals business, what widgets would we create?

Now we're way out of the box. We're not talking about performance appraisals anymore. And that's the key: We're not defining ourselves by our current widget. We are defining ourselves by the results we are here to accomplish. When we do that, every option is open to us.

Here, give it a try.

Insert the core widget of your agency and answer the five whys. Then pick an outcome level and come up with as many alternatives to your current widget that would better achieve that outcome.

Innovation Exercise

Why? So …

Why? So

Why? So

Why? So

Why? So

Widget: We produce a _____ for _____.
 (name of widget)   (name of end user)

Alternatives:

 BOX 5.5 **Myth 3: We're Not Here to Make a Profit**

Why it matters:

- To say we're not here to achieve a profit is akin to saying we're not here to achieve results.

- Profit (our outcomes) is the reason we exist—period. When we are not focused on results, we get bogged down with how we do things (our policies, procedures, and processes) and forget to ask why we are doing them in the first place.

continued

BOX 5.5

Myth 3: We're Not Here to Make a Profit
continued

- Our investors' (the taxpayers) primary concern is that we achieve the maximum return for the smallest investment. When we can't demonstrate results, we can't communicate with investors.

- Focusing on outcomes allows us to avoid becoming obsolete and, instead, encourages us to develop new and innovative ways of delivering results.

The truth:

We are here to make a profit—it's just not measured in dollars. Instead, it's measured in increased job creation, reduced recidivism, and higher quality of life. It's our responsibility to achieve a higher return for investors by making better widgets for customers in more efficient factories.

What to measure:

- Results customers achieve by using our widgets

- Results the organization achieves by customers using our widgets

  (Remember that outcomes tend to occur in a hierarchy. The trick is to measure the right level of outcome—choose too big an outcome and you'll have a hard time seeing any improvement or proving your contribution; choose too small and you limit your thinking.)

How to improve:

- Use five-whys thinking to define the true purpose for your widget.

- Ensure you are in the right business (laptops, not typewriters).

- Develop innovative alternatives to your existing widget, using five-why thinking, that could better meet each purpose.

- Work with customers to help design those new widgets.

- Build new, efficient factories to produce the new widgets.

- Involve employees in the improvement process.

Chapter 6

Making It Happen: Leading a Large-Scale Change Initiative

Now that the three myths have been removed, you can see that

1. We are here to achieve a profit and that we need to be as focused on our results as the private sector is focused on profit.

2. We do have customers; they may not be who we thought they were, but our success does depend on their satisfaction.

3. We do make widgets; we do have factories; and it is possible to measure, manage, and improve what we do.

The purpose of our organization, like any organization, is to achieve a higher return for investors by making better widgets for customers in more efficient factories. So how do we get started? First, let's get clear about what not to do.

Five Ways to Ruin Your Change Initiative

Focus Internally on Issues Like Communication and Employee Satisfaction

I have run across countless change initiatives that start with a steering team of managers and employees tasked with identifying the "issues" affecting the organization: morale, turnover, and communication. These well-meaning folks identify numerous internal concerns (synchronizing the time clocks, faster expense account processing, better company vehicles) and set about forming teams to work on these things.

Improve communication. Exactly what does this mean? People are quick to label all sorts of organizational dysfunction as "communication problems." Some of those dysfunctions include a horizontal process being managed by a vertical silo organization, a process with numerous handoffs, constant inspection, and no clear definitions of success. Other dysfunctions labeled communication problems include no interaction with the end-user customers or unresolved competing customer interests. More common dysfunctions labeled communication problems include a manager who paternalistically withholds so-called bad news, a staff member who is passed over for promotion, or coworkers who simply don't like each other. These latter situations are all quagmires to be avoided at all costs. You will endure much heartburn and have little or no impact on the outcome. Every improve-communication team since Gutenberg has come up with a newsletter as the solution. If they already have a newsletter, the team recommends putting it on the intranet. The answer to "improve communication" is not more communication. Poor communication is often the effect, not the cause, of a dysfunctional work system.

Increase employee satisfaction. I could go on and on about the reasons not to work on this. In many cases the reasons are the same as those listed for improving communication. Employee satisfaction is directly related to the science of motivation. Motivation is a science. There is a body of research that has validated what works and what does not. Unfortunately, team after team dabbles in this area with no understanding of what the research has identified. Nine times out of ten, the team recommends an employee-of-the-month program, more parties, and increased pay. Whether you fall in the behaviorist camp or the intrinsic-motivation camp, you can quickly see those solutions are hollow and ineffective. For a good synopsis of motivational theory, I refer you to Frederick Herzberg's seminal *Harvard Business Review* article on how to motivate employees.[1]

Rather than work on employee satisfaction, direct your improvement attention at the systems in the organization where those employees work. By fundamentally improving the systems that satisfy customers and that deliver organizational outcomes, you invariably end up improving the lives of the employees.

Better yet, focus the change initiative on customer satisfaction first. You will be amazed at the impact. During the course of improving things for customers, you inevitably improve things inside the organization. Further, by directing the attention outward, you avoid the petty bickering over inconsequential internal issues. Employees want to make their customers happy. Help them make that possible and you've got friends for life.

Give It a Name

What can possibly be wrong with naming your initiative? Think back to the graveyard of dead initiatives your organization has gone through. How many of them had names? The names are usually associated with the buzzwords of the era, like TQM, or MBO, or Performance Management. The problem with naming your change initiative is twofold:

It makes it a target. As much as we want everyone onboard with the changes we are making, they won't all be. Some people in this life are just miserable and are looking for something to blame their misery on. Usually they blame it on you and your crazy initiative. You'll notice this is happening when the employees change the name of the initiative. A large agency was replacing its new enterprise-wide administrative software package, called S.A.M., with a new and reputedly better version called S.A.M. 2. They printed banners, made T-shirts, and passed out mugs—all to get everyone excited about S.A.M. 2. By six months into the implementation, the employees had

---

[1] Frederick Herzberg, "One More Time: How Do You Motivate Employees?" *Harvard Business Review* 46 (January–February 1968).

changed the name of the initiative to Son of Sam, but they weren't allowed to make banners.

It makes it that other thing. When you give your initiative a name, you've just declared that it's an initiative; that is, it is something else that is not the core business. We have our day-to-day stuff to do, and then "that other thing." You'll often hear employees say, "I've got to go to one of those (insert name here) meetings." Improving the systems of our organizations should be part of what we do every day, not something else.

Too often we start our change initiatives with a big kickoff. We celebrate our intentions, not our results. Imagine if, on the morning of the Super Bowl, fans found the entire football team drunk in the parking lot celebrating that they were going to play in the Super Bowl that day. Whenever you launch your change initiative, save the banners and the mugs, and don't call it anything. When people ask what's going on, just reply, "We're trying to get better every day."

Pick Low-Hanging Fruit

Our natural inclination as we learn a new skill is to take baby steps until we are comfortable. Many organizational change initiatives take the same philosophy and start out applying new concepts on some "low-hanging fruit." The idea is to get some quick wins and build momentum. Only it doesn't work that way. By tackling small, perhaps easy things, it sets the expectation in the organization that this new initiative is not going to address anything important. Imagine standing in front of a room full of employees and declaring that we are going to radically improve our operations by 80 percent and we're going to start ... with the mailroom.

In addition, a quick win is usually neither a win nor quick. Managers' attention spans are relatively short, shorter than most change projects. All change takes at least six months no matter how small. (Don't believe me? How long would it take you to get a totally redesigned business card?) We might as well tackle the big stuff—the core systems most vital to achieving our results.

Train Everyone

Next we set about the hard work of training everyone. But training-driven change is built on two false assumptions:

- Individuals can change the system.

- Individuals will apply (successfully) what they learn.

Training-driven change was very popular in the TQM days. One state in our great Union trained all 60,000 state employees how to draw control charts. The effort yielded few results—no surprise. You can't train your way to change.

Assume Everyone Must Participate

Nearly all the energy in an initiative is spent creating it, naming it, celebrating its creation, forming our steering team, and training all employees, all for the purpose of "buy-in." We assume that everyone has to be onboard and everyone has to be doing "it." This is not a strategic way to make change.

So, What Should We Do?

Our approach to change has to be much more focused and strategic.

An organization I worked with developed a knockout leadership development program that turned middle managers into change agents. During the course of the program, these managers were leading teams in their work areas to improve customer satisfaction, streamline processes, and solve problems. They learned exactly what they needed to know to make system changes right when they needed them. They learned, for example, techniques for improving customer satisfaction, and before the next class convened a month later, they conducted focus groups with their end users. They learned by doing. Once the teams improved the systems in their work areas, they began working on removing the barriers to pride and joy in the workplace and developing employees' potential.

The program produced remarkable results. However, the program was not step 1 in the process. It came along eighteen months into the organization's improvement journey. It came along after the key systems in the organization had been improved and after folks had faith that the principles they were being taught could make a difference. The leadership development program was a means of expanding the initiative, not starting it.

The following are short- and long-term strategies to radically improve your organization.

Define the Desired Results (the Profit) for the Organization

Your organization may already have some kind of plan in place that provides direction. If you aren't sure your organization has one, look on some bookshelves or behind doors. You'll find one. It's usually the same size as your phone book; you just use it less.

Strategic plans should be focused. They are not designed to dictate the individual actions of every employee. Instead, they are there to say: "Here's how we see the future, here's the results we want to achieve, and here's what we're going to do differently to get them." It makes little sense to write a strategic plan that explains what you already do.

A good strategic plan should describe clearly the success measures and list three to five priorities for improvement.

Identify the Key Systems (the Widgets) Most Vital to Achieving the Results

I live by the motto that it's not important that we do everything well, but that we do the really important things really well. Or, as Archbishop Oscar Romero is said to have put it, "We cannot do everything, and there is a sense of liberation in realizing that. This enables us to do something, and to do it very well."[2] Of all the factories producing all the widgets in your organization, some are more critical than others. How do we know which ones are the most vital? The ones that have the biggest impact on your results.

Change happens in projects. If you want great change, run great projects. Reading a book or attending a workshop may help change thinking, but projects are the way we change the work. After we identify our most vital systems, we charter projects to radically improve them. For the purposes of selecting some high-impact projects, we want to consider systems that

- are the largest consumers of the organization's time and money

- are a source of customer dissatisfaction

- are a source of errors and rework

- could benefit from going 80 percent faster

---

[2] From the "Prayer of Oscar Romero," delivered by John Cardinal Dearden, November 1979, and drafted by Ken Untener.

- will have a big impact on other systems in the organization

- will yield a high return on the project's investment

- will show noticeable improvement within 12 months' time.[3]

Some additional rules of thumb:

- Cross-functional widgets provide the best opportunities for improvement.

- If the project doesn't deal with a widget or a process, it's not going to be easy to get your arms around it.

- The project can focus on a widget that does not yet exist; that is, the lack of a certain widget or system may be what's holding the organization back.

Form Teams to Improve the Key Systems

Every success story in this book was created by a cross-functional team of employees working on improving a system. Employees, working on the right thing (a system) with the right help (a trained change agent) and the full support of an executive sponsor can come up with amazing results. Depending on the scope of the project, teams may work on any or all of the components of the system-of-work model.

Teams may focus on streamlining the factory and finding the 80 percent time savings. They may use data and problem-solving techniques to eliminate errors and rework. They may use voice-of-the-customer techniques to determine customer priorities and improve the widget. Or they may focus on the outcome and come up with completely new ways of doing things.

Two ingredients are critical to a team's success: a supportive management sponsor and a trained change agent. The management sponsor is the individual with the authority to say yes to a team's recommendations. The management sponsor sets the scope and boundaries up front and is the person the team pitches its ideas to at

[3] Criteria are adapted from Robin L. Lawton, *Creating a Customer-Centered Culture: Leadership in Quality, Innovation, and Speed* (Milwaukee, Wis.: ASQC Quality Press, 1993), chap. 7, "Implementation," www.imtC3.com.

the end. During the project, the sponsor is available to remove road-blocks the team may encounter.

Change agents are individuals who have the knowledge, skills, and tools to help organizations radically improve. Rarely in a position of authority, they achieve results with their keen ability to facilitate groups of people through well-defined processes to develop, organize, and sell new ideas. They challenge teams to think outside the box and use innovative tools to harness that creativity to make improvements that matter to the bottom line. Change agents are a leader's best friend. For more information on change agents consult my book, *The Change Agent's Guide to Radical Improvement*.

Expanding the Initiative

The process described above can be repeated time and again until your organization has exhausted its key systems. That is, repeat the process until the core business—the systems most vital to the organization's results—has been identified, dramatically improved, and continuously measured and planned for. Many organizations choose to use this selection process as part of their annual strategic planning. The following diagram shows the leadership system of an organization that won a State Quality Award. If you are familiar with the Malcolm Baldrige criteria for performance excellence, you will be familiar with the tight integration of the strategic planning, customer satisfaction, information and analysis, process management, and results categories.

Leadership System—Continuous Improvement of Systems

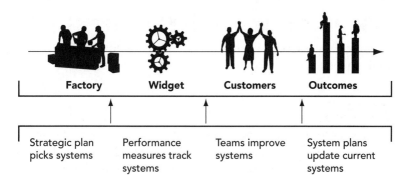

Factory	Widget	Customers	Outcomes
Strategic plan picks systems	Performance measures track systems	Teams improve systems	System plans update current systems

The strategic plan identifies the systems most vital to carrying out the organization's strategy and achieving its results. Teams are formed to improve each key system that is picked—streamlining the factory, reducing errors, increasing customer satisfaction, and increasing results. A balanced set of performance measures are developed to track efficiency, effectiveness, and customer satisfaction. The "system owner" is responsible for reporting on these performance measures regularly and for developing an annual system plan that identifies the systems' goals and how they will be met.

As you expand, focus capacity building on change agents, top management, teams, and middle management, in that order. Change agents are the biggest constraint to the success of change initiatives because either there aren't enough of them or they do not have the skills to do the job. Change agents are often the coaches to the top-management team. Investing in them first takes you a long way toward improving the performance of the top-management team. Before any teams are formed, top management should understand the philosophy and methods associated with the change initiative, that is, they should no longer believe the three myths, and they should understand the basic methods for improving systems. Once there is success and the organization trusts that the change initiative is a positive thing, invest in the middle managers. They too need to be able to see past the myths and believe in what is possible. You can make some significant changes without their buy-in, but you will never sustain change without them. Many change initiatives stall once they get to the middle managers. You need a way to engage their hearts and minds and convert them into change agents.

Long-Term Strategy for Radical Improvement

For long-term success, change has to come about at three levels: inside the whole organization, at the level of the system, and within each individual staff member.

Organization Level
Many keys to the long-term success of any change initiative are at the organizational level. At some point, system changes will not be enough to ensure the long-term viability of the enterprise. To sup-

Three Levels Necessary for Success

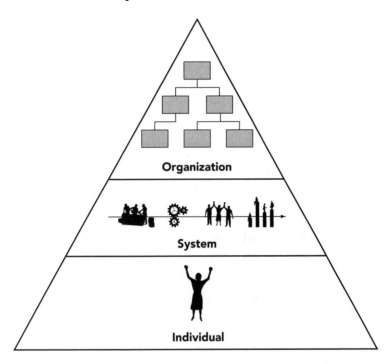

plement targeted system changes, you will likely need to do the following:

Ensure DNA of change is present in the organization. The organization needs a balanced set of metrics that it can use for analysis, planning, and celebration. These metrics should give the leadership team a comprehensive view of how well the organization is performing on its priorities. In addition, the organization needs some leading or predictive metrics in order to see the future better. You can't lead an organization by always looking in the rearview mirror. Although many organizations have metrics, often they don't do anything meaningful with them. For each measure there needs to be a process for receiving feedback, setting goals, creating plans, and reviewing progress. The absence of any of these components leads to stalled progress. Measurement is merely a tool to start a discussion. Without the discussion, the measurement is meaningless. Without a plan, the discussion is meaningless.

Adjust structure to align responsibility and authority and to accommodate new process designs. At some point, the structure of the organization will become the main constraint to further improvement. (This point is usually not at the beginning of the change initiative.) New process designs may dictate new structures and new jobs. Old organizational divisions may not make sense anymore. Performance measures might reveal a disconnect between what someone is accountable for and what that person has the power to change. These are times to adjust the organizational structure. When changing the structure, remember three things: communicate, communicate, and communicate. Let people know why you're doing it, when you're doing it, what will change, what will not change, and how it affects them personally. And communicate all of this even before you're done! The organization will find it has made large withdrawals in its trust account if people feel that they didn't have a role in the change or that it was done behind their backs. Structural changes should be done with people, not to them.

Develop executives. Surprise! The current change initiative you're working on will not be the last one or even the best one. It shouldn't

DNA of Change

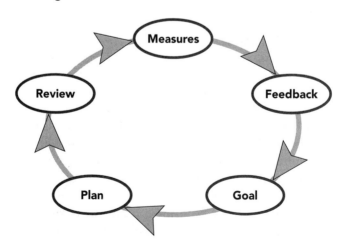

be. The organization should be continuously learning, continuously searching for better ways to do things. If the executives aren't learning, chances are the organization isn't either. Executives are busy people, but that is no excuse. And, while you're developing executives, also develop future executives.

System Level

Sustaining system-level change for the long term involves continuous attention and strategic expansion. The effort shifts from creating dramatic performance improvements to sustaining the gains with incremental improvements over time. Improvement efforts cascade down to the processes and subsystems that feed the key systems. After my team improved the tax refund process at a state agency, for example, we identified numerous subsystems as needing improvements, including how funds were transferred and how the forms were designed as well as how the computer system was maintained. Several key elements sustain and enhance system-level change:

Ensure that DNA of change is present for each key system. Improvement is not a one-time event. It's a continuous process. Even if you have already radically improved a key system, you need a mechanism to continuously improve it for the long haul. The DNA of change is critical for this. Key systems in the organization should have a balanced set of metrics that encompass every aspect of the system-of-work model: customer satisfaction, effectiveness, efficiency, and employee satisfaction. Regular review cycles, goal setting, and planning will help ensure the system is better tomorrow than it is today.

Benchmark and stretch. So by now you're pretty good. Are you the best? A great way to achieve the next breakthrough is to get outside the organization and see who's better than you and why. Don't limit yourself to your industry. Similar factories exist in state prisons, patient billing centers, consulting firms, and the Ford Motor Company. Some of the best ideas come from the strangest places. A progressive organization I worked with required each system to find the best in their industry and the best in another industry to benchmark with. Their performance helped set higher expectations, and the field trips produced new ideas and better ways of doing things.

Turn managers into change agents. The role of managers is to continuously improve the system for the betterment of the organization, its customers, and its employees. These people are not paid to keep employees from stealing the furniture. Managers need to know how to change the systems for which they are responsible. All managers should know how to

- determine customer expectations
- develop performance measures
- analyze data
- improve a process
- solve a problem
- manage a project
- develop their people.

Individual Level

Individual-level change is a subject that requires a book of its own. In fact, there already are countless books on the topic. There are numerous theories, many of them competing, but all with something to add to the discussion. I will not pretend to give you the solution for developing individual performance. Instead, I will direct you to the sources that I have found provide the greatest insight and inspiration:

- *The Leader's Handbook,* by Peter Scholtes (1998)
- "One More Time: How Do You Motivate Employees?" by Frederick Herzberg in *Harvard Business Review,* (January–February 1968)
- *Zapp! The Lightning of Empowerment,* by William Byham (with Jeff Cox) (1998)

At the heart of my philosophy of individual-level change are two principles:

- Fix the system first.
- Focus on people's intrinsic motivation.

Here are some basics necessary to sustain change at the individual level:

Ensure DNA of change is present for each work unit as well as for individuals, when appropriate. I hate to sound like a broken record but this is crucial. People work all day. They would like to know how they are doing. It is incumbent on managers to share with their employees some critical elements:

- the big picture and the employees' place in it[4]

- the long- and short-term goals of the unit and how those goals apply to them

- the values of the organization and what that means for them

- how the unit is performing (and it never hurts to seek employees' ideas on how to make it better)

Weekly staff meetings should be about more than dress-code policies and doughnut ceremonies. Where are we headed, how are we doing, what can we do differently? The emphasis should be on the unit or the system.

In addition, employees may want to have their own goals. If they want a manager's help in setting them, great. If not, don't. It doesn't have to be the manager's guidance and feedback that develops an employee. Teach them how to use the DNA of change and then get out of the way.

Redesign jobs and training to accommodate new process designs. Nothing can be more frustrating for employees than to change the system but not be provided with the new skills to succeed in the new job. New processes typically lead to more advanced jobs. People need the time and attention to adapt.

Provide career development opportunities for those who want them. Not everybody is in the rat race. Some people want to keep doing what they do forever. Let them. But make sure that is a choice they

---

[4] Lee Iacocca said this before I did.

are making and not their only option. For those who want to advance in their careers, show them the resources to do it. Build career paths. Make visible the skills necessary to hold different jobs in the organization. Invest in training for the job they have and the job they want to have. If they ask, help them find a job that better suits their interests. Too many managers want to make their units like the former East Germany. They want to build a giant wall around their units to make sure nobody defects. The result is what you saw in East Germany: people with little motivation, passion, or hope for their lives. Good managers know that the goal is not to get the most work out of people but to help people get the most out of work.

Involve employees in change efforts. People support what they help create. Never stop asking for help.

Provide the fuel for long-term change initiatives. All long-term changes need a steady supply of fuel. Accomplishment and celebration are the fuels that keep people going.

Finally ...

I hope this book has opened the door to what's possible for your agency. That's all I was trying to do. Once you get past the myth that government is different, so much good stuff is out there that you can use now, right away: All the best business methods for customer satisfaction, efficiency, and innovation can be applied because you have widgets, factories, customers, and results. It is our beliefs that hold us back. And it is our beliefs that can make us great.

- Plant a thought, reap an action
- Plant an action, reap a habit
- Plant a habit, reap a character
- Plant a character, reap a destiny.

I wish you the very best of luck on your journey.

Appendix

Critical Components for a Customer-Centered Culture

The following are the critical components necessary to create a customer-centered culture, as introduced in Robin Lawton's groundbreaking 1993 book, *Creating a Customer-Centered Culture: Leadership in Quality, Innovation and Speed:*

1. **Redefining service as tangible products.** At the height of the Total Quality Management movement, nearly every organization was trying to apply the Industrial Age concepts manufacturers were using to build quality, defect-free widgets. The problem was that many of these companies were in the service business. While many quality professionals struggled with the concept of service quality, Lawton introduced the concept of defining service as a tangible product. This new way of thinking helped overcome the problems with the traditional way of thinking about service. The term *service* lacks any shared meaning, is reactive in nature, and focuses our attention on activities and process, not what customers want. Defining service as tangible products helps focus our attention on what customers care about—what we are going to give them that helps them achieve their desired outcomes.

2. **Defining customers by their roles.** "Who is the customer?" is a debate that rages inside and outside of government. While most organizations were content to categorize customers as internal or external, Lawton crystallized the true conflict by identifying the often-competing customer roles of end users and brokers. End users are the customers who actually use products to achieve a desired outcome. Brokers do not use the product themselves but transfer it to someone else who will use it. Although both customer groups may be important, our focus should be on meeting the desires of end users. Unfortunately, as Lawton pointed out, brokers tend to have the most power over the way things are done. This occurs either because we fail to understand the differentiation or because the brokers have position or control of the purse strings. Regardless, end users always win in the long run, often to the detriment of the organization. Successful organizations will work to understand the needs of all their customers but will strive to put the desires of end users first. Lawton has also been a longtime advocate of proactive customer satisfaction—working with end users up front to design excellent products rather than relying on reactive customer surveys to determine how well products are doing.

3. **Concentrating on outcome-focused innovation.** One of Lawton's most important contributions has been the clear focus on outcomes as the source of innovation, particularly customer outcomes. These outcomes (like health, confidence, and improved quality of life) are stable over time, but customer loyalties are not. Simply put, customers are loyal to the products that best enable them to achieve their outcomes. Organizations that are truly customer centered will seek to create value by focusing on achieving customer outcomes first, before they worry about product quality or process performance. What good is it to make something absolutely perfect that the customer does not want?

To learn more about Robin Lawton and customer-centered culture, visit www.imtC3.com.

Index

Note: Page numbers followed by *n* indicate notes.

Key system identification, 107–109
Knowledge work, 52

Law enforcement, 65–66
Lawton, Robin L., 7, 30, 30*n*, 63,
    63*n*, 79*n*, 97, 97*n*, 108*n*, 117,
    118
The Leader's Handbook (Scholtes), 2*n*,
    20*n*, 114
Leadership development, 106,
    112–113
Leadership system, 110–111
Lean manufacturing, 39
Legislators, 87
Legislature, 61
Libraries, 94
License plate, 64–66
Long-term strategy, 110–116

Management sponsor, 108–109
Managers, 114
Master of business administration
    (MBA), 11
Master of public administration
    (MPA), 11
Measurement
    outcome, 89–93
    performance, 80
    process, 83, 100–101, 112
    role of, 39–44, 111
    system-of-work, 4
Motivation, 20–23, 37, 40, 103–104
Motivation theory, 104
Myths, 5–11

Negative reinforcement, 20–21
Nursing home license, 68

Obsolescence, 95–96
Organizational charts, 15
Organizational-level change, 110–113
Organizations, 6, 9
Outcomes, 7, 89–93, 118
Output, 34

PalmPilot, 96
Pay-for-performance, 6
Performance appraisals, 6, 18, 97–98
Performance improvement, 24–25
Performance management, 6, 18
Performance measures, 80, 109

Personal development plans, 18
Petronious Arbiter, 17
Plant manager, 38–39
Politburo, 14–15
Positive reinforcement, 20–21
Power, 69
Prevention programs, 93
Privatization, 82
Process, 34
Profit, 85
Purpose, 7

Quality function deployment, 39
Quality principles, 44
Quick wins, 105

Radio, 64
Reengineering, 39
Reform initiatives, 12–25
Reforms, 26
Regulators, 66–68
Reorganization, 15–18
Review process, 111, 112, 113

Satisfaction measures, 70–84
Scholtes, Peter R., 2, 2*n*, 20, 20*n*, 43,
    114
Service, 35–37, 71, 117
Service integration, 79
"Show Me Results" system, 14–15
SIPOC model, 7
Six Sigma, 39, 81
Social services, 72
Special-cause variation, 42
Stalk, George, Jr., 47*n*
Step-by-step focus group process, 77
Strategic planning, 107, 109
Streamlining, 108
Stuckey's, 95, 96
Student syndrome, 49–50
Suggestion systems, 18
Supply-chain management, 39
System of work, 6–9
    areas of emphasis in, 31
    communicating value in, 87–88
    food stamp distribution, 29
    foster care subsidies, 29
    Medicaid reimbursement, 28
    plant manager tasks in, 38–39
    purpose and, 7
System-of-work measures, 4

About the Author

Ken Miller is the founder of the Change and Innovation Agency, a firm dedicated to helping its clients radically improve. Earlier, when Ken was deputy director of the Missouri Department of Revenue, he led the effort to transform the agency from one responsible for collecting taxes and licensing cars and drivers into a State Quality Award winner. Only a handful of government agencies in the country receive such a distinction. Ken was then named director of performance improvement for the state government of Missouri. Missouri later became one of only two states to receive a grade of A for managing for results from *Governing* magazine. Before he joined the Department of Revenue, Ken was a partner in the customer satisfaction consulting firm of International Management Technologies; the firm's clients included Motorola, Raytheon, AT&T, Eastman Kodak, 3M, Microsoft, Northwest Airlines, and the U.S. Department of Defense.

Ken was named one of the country's top change agents by *Fast Company* magazine (the judging panel included Tom Peters). He has worked with committed and enthusiastic people in tough environments to tackle some big issues:

- How can we best organize the resources of a community to fight poverty?

- How can we bring the radical improvements of manufacturing to the 86 percent of the workforce that doesn't make widgets?

- How can we get union workers in psychiatric facilities to say "Thank God It's Monday"?

- How can we overcome the barriers that prevent most inner-city kids from going to college?

- How do we make a child abuse hotline as responsive and reliable as 9-1-1?

- Where's my tax refund?

- Why is this DMV line so brutally long?

Ken's first book, *The Change Agent's Guide to Radical Improvement,* was published in 2002 and is available from ASQC Quality Press. To learn more about Ken and find free resources to support this book, please visit www.changeagents.info or www.wedontmakewidgets. com.